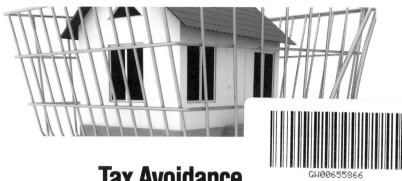

Tax Avoidance
the Property Investor

GW00655866

THE COMPLEMENTARY WEBSITE

The http://books.indicator.co.uk website gives you instant access to all the ready-to-use documents, tools, policies, etc. that complement this publication.

Go to

http://books.indicator.co.uk

and enter your access code
UAH925

THE CD-ROM

Don't have access to the Internet?
Call Customer Services on 01233 653500 to request a CD-ROM.

ISBN 978-1-906892-52-4

Fifth Edition - First Print - E05P1

Introduction

Despite the recent lack of capital growth, the current low interest rates have continued to make property investing very attractive with rental profits providing a better return for many than the stock market or savings accounts.

But of course where there's an opportunity to make higher rental profits, there's an opportunity for the Taxman to come along and grab a slice. So property investing means the need for some serious tax planning if you want to keep the Taxman's take to an absolute minimum.

In this book, Tax Avoidance for the Property Investor, we've considered how all the relevant taxes might come together. In plain English, we've suggested 100% legal and legitimate ways to avoid those taxes. So we've done all the hard work for you - whether you're a seasoned investor or a first-time buyer, you'll find a stack of ready-to-use tax avoidance strategies in these pages. Go ahead and try them - you've nothing to lose but a whole load of tax to save.

Catherine Hamilton-Woodthorpe

May 2012

Table of contents

Section I - Avoiding tax on rental income

Table of contents

Section II - Avoiding tax on property disposals

6.   The tax implications of gifting properties   65

Section III - Buying strategies to avoid tax

Section IV - Overseas property tax issues

Table of contents

Section V - Appendices

SECTION I

Avoiding tax on rental income

1. Rental income - the tax basics

1.1. INCOME TAX RATES

As a property investor, you have to pay income tax on the net rental income you receive on an annual basis. The amount depends on your total income for the year. The table below shows the income tax rates for 2012/13 for an individual with the standard personal allowance of £8,105:

INCOME BAND	RATE	NOTES
£0 - £8,105	0%	No tax payable under £8,105
£8,106 - £42,475	20%	Maximum tax payable at this level of income = £6,874
£42,476 - £100,000	40%	Pay 40p in every £1 on next £57,525 of income
£100,001 - £116.210	60%	Effectively pay 60p in every £1 on the next £16,210 income due to withdrawal of personal allowance which is reduced by £1 for every £2 income over £100,000
£116,211 - £150,000	40%	Pay 40p in every £1 on the next £33,790
Over £150,000	50%	Pay 50p in every £1 of income over £150,000

The rates for previous years can be found at http://www.hmrc.gov.uk/rates/it.htm.

2012 Budget. It was announced in the 2012 Budget that, with effect from April 6 2013, there will be a cut in the rate for those earning over £150,000 from 50% to 45%.

EXAMPLE

Valerie receives an annual salary of £34,000 and has paid £5,179 in PAYE on this. She also has net rental profits of £10,000 for the year. Therefore, Valerie's total income is £44,000 and her total tax liability is £7,484 (£44,000 - £42,475 = £1,525 x 40% = £610 + £6,874). The additional tax she will have to pay on her rental income is £2,305 (£7,484 less £5,179).

Non-taxpayer

If your total income for the year, including rental income, is under £8,105 then you have no tax to pay.

Basic rate taxpayer

This is where your other income for the year is less than £42,475. Assuming rental income doesn't take you over the £42,475 threshold, it will be taxed at 20%.

Higher rate taxpayer

In this case, your other income for the year is between £42,475 and £150,000. Assuming net rental income doesn't take you over the £150,000 threshold, it will be taxed at 40%. The exception is where your other income is between £100,000 and £116,210 when your rental income will effectively be taxed at 60% due to the loss of the personal allowance which is reduced by £1 for every £2 income over £100,000. For simplicity, when referring to a higher rate taxpayer in this book, we mean a 40% taxpayer.

Additional rate taxpayer

In this case, your other income for the year is more than £150,000. This means that your rental income will be taxed at 50%.

1.2. HOW DO I WORK OUT RENTAL PROFITS (OR LOSSES!)?

For income tax purposes, property investment is treated as a business and, therefore, net rental income is calculated in broadly the same way as self-employed business profits. To work out your net rental profits, you need to take your gross rental income in the year and subtract any ongoing, property-related expenses. See Chapter 2 for details of the expenses you can claim against income.

EXAMPLE

Jenny receives monthly rental income of £500 from her investment property. The property is let for the whole of the 2012/13 tax year, so she has annual rental income of £6,000. Her property-related expenses were interest on the buy-to-let mortgage of £3,600 and £80 for the annual gas safety certificate. So, Jenny's taxable rental profit is £2,320 (£6,000 - (£3,600 + £80)). If Jenny is a higher rate taxpayer, then her additional tax bill will be £928 (£2,320 x 40%).

1.2.1. Do I need to prepare a set of accounts?

If you own (or owned) a property and earned rent from it during the period April 6 2012 to April 5 2013, then you ought to prepare an income and expenditure account to establish whether or not you have made a taxable profit or loss for that year. However, these accounts do not need to be submitted to the Taxman - just keep them for your records and to help you complete your tax return.

Download Zone

For an interactive calculator, visit **http://books.indicator.co.uk**. You'll find the access code on page 2 of this book.

1.2.2. I've got two UK properties, do I need to prepare two sets of accounts?

If you have more than one UK property, then this is generally treated as a single property business. Therefore, you only need to complete one set of accounts, adding together the rental income and expenses from all the properties.

Exception: Furnished holiday accommodation

If you've got income from furnished holiday accommodation, this has special tax rules and needs to be shown separately (see 3.2 for more on the income tax treatment of furnished holiday accommodation). Since 2009/10, properties in the European Economic Area (EEA) also qualify as furnished holiday accommodation. All the furnished holiday accommodation that you own in the UK is taxed as one business and all the properties you own in other EEA states are taxed as a separate business. You will, therefore, need to keep separate records for each business. Unlike other overseas property (see below), EEA furnished holiday accommodation profits or losses are entered on a separate page of the "UK Property" pages on your tax return.

Exception: Overseas property

Any overseas property that you let out needs to be shown separately from the rental income from the UK properties (with the exception of furnished holiday accommodation in the EEA as explained above). Due to the different tax regimes in different countries, it is advisable to prepare one set of accounts for each country that you have properties in (see 12.2 for details of how overseas rental property is taxed).

1.2.3. Can I choose the accounting date?

The accounting period for all rental income is the tax year, i.e. April 6 to the following April 5. You can prepare accounts to a different year-end (e.g. January 1 to December 31), but the profits would then have to be apportioned to work out the profits for the year to April 5. So, unless you have strong, non-tax reasons for doing so, it would be advisable to prepare accounts to April 5 each year.

1.2.4. How long should I keep the records for?

You must keep records of your rental income and expenses for at least five years and ten months from the end of the tax year. So, your records for the year-ended April 5 2013 need to be kept until January 31 2019.

1.2.5. What happens if I've "lost" the records?

There's nothing to worry about, unless you have an enquiry from the Taxman. As with all tax laws, ignorance of the rules regarding the keeping of records is no excuse and, in theory, the Taxman could decide to charge a penalty for not keeping proper records. This could be up to £3,000 a year. However, this rarely happens in practice.

However, during an enquiry, if you can't produce records to back up your expenses then the Taxman will use his "best judgement" and disallow those items that he feels are incorrect. This could lead to you having to make an additional payment of tax plus interest. On top of that, the Taxman could charge you a penalty for "careless inaccuracies" in the return which could be up to 100% of the additional tax due. This is because he views not keeping accurate records as careless.

1.2.6. When should I account for rental income? When it is due or when it is actually received?

The general rule is that you should account for rental income and expenses when they are due (the "accruals" basis) rather than when they are received or paid (the "cash" basis).

Exception

If your gross rental receipts are less than £15,000 a year (£1,250 a month), then you are allowed to account for rental income and expenses on a "cash" basis, i.e. when you actually receive the rent or pay the bills (see http://www.hmrc.gov.uk/manuals/pimmanual/pim1101.htm).

Which method should I use?

Even if your rental receipts are less than £15,000, if you receive rents in advance and pay expenses in arrears, it would be beneficial for you to account for rental income using the "accruals" basis.

EXAMPLE

Greg started renting a property on January 1 2013, at a monthly rent of £800, which the tenant pays in advance. Therefore, by April 5 2013, Greg has received four lots of £800 (£3,200). However, the last payment of £800 relates to the whole month of April. Under the "accruals" basis, Greg would include only £133 of this (£800 x 5 days/30 days) in his rental income calculation this year. If he used the "cash" basis, he would have to include the full £800. As a higher rate taxpayer, using the "accruals" basis has saved him £267 in 2012/13.

1.3. WHICH TAX RETURNS MUST I COMPLETE IF I HAVE RENTAL INCOME?

UK property

You need to complete a self-assessment tax return that incorporates "UK Property" supplementary pages, UKP1 and UKP2. These pages cover all types of rental income, whether it is from numerous properties or a single rental. If you have income from the commercial letting of furnished holiday accommodation in the UK then you need to complete UKP1. For all other UK rental income, you need to complete UKP2.

Overseas property

Any income from overseas land and property should not be included on the "UK Property" pages. This income should be included on the "Foreign" supplementary pages, F4 and F5. The only exception to this is income from the commercial letting of furnished holiday accommodation in the EEA which you need to enter on a separate "UK Property" page UKP1.

Jointly-held property

Each owner must include their share of the rental income and expenses on their own tax return. You do not need to complete a partnership tax return.

1.3.1. Where do I get the returns from?

If you have been sent a paper tax return without the "UK Property" supplementary pages, you can download the additional pages from the Taxman's website (http://www.hmrc.gov.uk/sa/forms/content.htm).

If you complete your tax return online, then you can use the Taxman's free tax return software to complete the "UK Property" pages.

1.3.2. By when do I need to submit the return?

The deadline for submission of self-assessment tax returns is October 31 following the end of the tax year if you send in a paper return or January 31 following the end of the tax year if you file your return online. So, the tax return showing the rental income received in the year to April 5 2013 will need to be submitted to the Taxman by January 31 2014 as long as you submit your return online. There is an automatic £100 penalty for a late return whether or not you have additional tax to pay.

First-time investor

If this is the first year that you have received rental income, then, theoretically, you should advise the Taxman of your new source of income by October 5 of the following tax year. In practice, however, you won't incur any penalties as long as you submit a tax return showing the new source of income by January 31 the following year.

1.3.3.   When do I pay the tax?

You need to pay any additional tax that you owe to the Taxman by January 31 following the tax year. So, for the tax year-ended April 5 2013, you need to pay the additional tax by January 31 2014. You will be charged interest on late payments.

If you owe more than £1,000 (and the additional tax is more than 20% of your total tax liability for the year), then as well as the additional tax, you also have to pay a further 50% on top. You then have to make another 50% payment by July 31. The two 50% payments are "payments on account" of the following tax year and will be taken off next year's tax bill.

EXAMPLE

David had rental income and his additional tax liability for the year-ended April 5 2013 was £1,500. David's total tax liability for the year was £5,000 and he had paid £3,500 tax on his only other income, a private pension, at source through the PAYE system. Therefore, as the additional tax is more than £1,000 and more than 20% of his total tax liability, David has to make the following payments:

By January 31 2014

2012/13 tax liability	£1,500	
2013/14 first "payment on account"	£750	(50% of £1,500)
Total	£2,250	

By July 31 2014

2013/14 second "payment on account"	£750	

In the following tax year (2013/14), David's tax liability is £1,600. Therefore, David will make the following payments:

By January 31 2015

2013/14 balancing payment	£100	(£1,600 less the two
	£750	"payments on account")
2014/15 first "payment on account"	£800	
Total	£900	

By July 31 2015

2014/15 second "payment on account"	£800	

Note. As you can see, when you receive rental income for the first time, your initial tax bill could be substantially more than you've estimated due to the fact that you've effectively tax to pay on two years worth of profits in the first year. However, there is a way around this problem:

Tip

If your additional tax liability is less than £3,000 and you submit your paper tax return by October 31, this amount will be collected through your PAYE code (assuming you're employed or receiving a pension) in the following tax year. If you file your return online, the deadline is later - December 30.

This means that a 2012/13 underpayment will be collected by monthly instalments between April 2014 and March 2015, rather than as a single payment on January 31 2014. This also eliminates payments on account in 2014.

1.3.4. Can I complete the returns myself or do I need an accountant?

There's no requirement to employ an accountant. However, if you have several properties, then it could be cost-effective. An accountant will usually charge between £350 and £750 plus VAT to complete your rental income accounts and tax eturn depending on the number of properties you own.

1.4. RENT-A-ROOM RELIEF

If you generate extra income by letting a room (which must be furnished) in your own home to a lodger then you can claim a special relief called "rent-a-room". Under this relief, you can earn up to £4,250 tax-free. The letting must be for residential purposes and not, for example, used exclusively as office accommodation. The lodger will typically have a furnished bedroom and share the use of other rooms, although they could occupy an entire floor of your home. You can choose to take advantage of the rent-a-room scheme, regardless of whether you own your own home or rent it. However, if you are renting, you should check whether your lease allows you to take a lodger.

1.4.1. Gross rent less than £4,250

If the total amount you receive in a year from letting part of your house, including charges for meals, cleaning, laundry and goods and services of a similar nature, is less than £4,250, there's no tax to pay. However, this means that if you elect for rent-a-room, any loss you make would also not be allowable.

Even if you receive rent-a-room income of less than £4,250 a year (£81 a week), make sure you add up your expenses. If they work out as more than your income, i.e. you've made a loss, elect not to apply rent-a-room for a particular year of assessment and include the rental income with your other property income (the "strict" method). The election must be made within twelve months after the January 31 following the tax year. For example, for the 202/13 tax year, an election must be made by January 31 2015. You can then offset the losses against any other rental income you receive in the current or subsequent tax years. It's possible to switch between the "rent-a-room" relief and the "strict" method from year to year if you wish.

If you want to apply the rent-a-room exemption, put an X in Box 4 on page UKP1 of the tax return. If you want to elect not to apply the exemption, simply don't put an X in Box 4! In other words, unlike some elections, you don't need to write a separate letter to the Taxman.

1.4.2.   Gross rent more than £4,250

If your total rent-a-room receipts are more than £4,250, then, by default, you will be taxed on your rental income less expenses.

However, you can elect to be taxed as if the profit from the letting is equal to the difference between the total gross rents receivable and £4,250. In this case, no deduction is given for expenses.

This election must also be made within twelve months from January 31 following the end of the tax year and will continue to have effect until withdrawn. Again, it's easy to make the election - don't put an X in Box 4 on page UKP1 of your tax return. Instead, enter your rental income in Box 20 and the rent-a-room exemption (£4,250) as expenses in Box 37 "Rent a Room exempt amount".

TɪP

If your income is more than £4,250 and your expenses are less than £4,250, then make this election.

Exᴀᴍᴘʟᴇ 1

Lisa lets two rooms in her house for £50 a week each (£5,200 a year). She has related expenses of £1,500, so her profit is £3,700. By default, Lisa will be taxed on her income (£5,200) less expenses (£1,500), £3,700.

However, if Lisa elects to just be taxed on her rental income over £4,250, then she will only be taxed on £950 (£5,200 less £4,250) - a tax saving of £1,100 for a higher rate taxpayer.

EXAMPLE 2

Frankie lets two rooms in her house for £80 a week each (£8,320 a year). However, she has related expenses of £4,800. By default, Frankie will be taxed on her income less expenses, i.e. £3,520. If Frankie had made an election, she would have been taxed on the higher figure of £4,070 (£8,320 less £4,250).

1.4.3. Is the £4,250 per person or per property?

If you own a property jointly, the £4,250 has to be halved, i.e. £2,125 each. But it's interesting to note that the Taxman hasn't specified what happens if three or more individuals own a house in which they all live. From his guidance, it would seem that each of them has a limit of £2,125.

1.4.4. Can more than one room be let?

The rent-a-room relief applies to any proportion of the property that you live in, so renting out more than one room would qualify (as long as each room is furnished). However, the £4,250 tax-free allowance is fixed regardless of the number of rooms let out. The relief can even extend to the letting of a self-contained flat as long as the division of the property is only temporary.

1.4.5. Do I have to live in the property?

You must occupy the property as your main home at the same time as the lodger for at least part of the letting period in each tax year. This means that as long as there is an overlap between you living in the property and the lodger being there, you can move out for the rest of the tax year.

2. Reduce your rental income by maximising expenses

2.1. WHAT COSTS CAN I DEDUCT FROM MY RENTAL INCOME?

As mentioned in 1.2., as with other businesses, you are able to offset property-related expenditure against the gross rents you receive. Therefore, to reduce the amount of rental profit and, consequently, the amount of tax you pay, you need to claim as many expenses as possible. However, in order for the Taxman to allow the expenditure, it has to obey the following rules:

"Wholly and exclusively"

This means that you cannot deduct an expense that is used partly for the property and partly for another purpose UNLESS the property proportion of that "mixed" expense can be separately identified.

EXAMPLE

Steve is refurbishing his own home and his investment property. He goes to a DIY store and buys ten boxes of floor tiles for £200. He uses four on his own property and six on the investment property. Therefore, he can claim 6/10ths of £200 against his rental income.

Steve also pays a cleaner £50 a week (£2,600 a year) for ten hours' work. The cleaner spends two hours a week at Steve's own home and eight hours cleaning his investment properties. Therefore, Steve can deduct £2,080 (8/10ths of £2,600) against his rental income.

Paid by you

Only expenses that are actually paid by you can be offset against your rental income. For example, if it is your tenant's responsibility to pay the Council Tax and TV licence, then you cannot deduct these expenses from the rental income you receive.

Not capital

Deciding on whether costs are capital is a grey area. Even the Taxman admits it is "far from easy". Basically, costs that you incur in the day-to-day running of your property investment business are not capital expenses and can be deducted from your rental income. However, costs incurred in significantly improving your property are considered capital and cannot be deducted.

NOTE. Although the capital costs cannot be deducted against your rental income, they can be deducted from your sale proceeds when you sell the property (see 4.2.3.).

So as long as you can prove that the expenditure meets the above rules, you can claim it. On the following pages, we look more in depth at the typical expenses you can deduct from your rental income.

2.2. INTEREST CHARGES

Buying a property to rent out usually involves some level of borrowing. You can offset the interest paid on these loans against your rental income.

2.2.1. What is meant by interest charges?

Interest charges are the amounts you pay back to a lender which are above and beyond the initial amount that you borrowed.

2.2.2. Which types of interest can I claim?

The general rule is that you can claim interest on any loans that are incurred for the purposes of the property investment. Whether the loan interest is an allowable deduction doesn't depend on which property the loan is secured on, but rather on what the loan funds are used for.

Interest on a mortgage on the investment property

Most property investors don't have the funds to purchase properties outright. Instead, they take out a mortgage to buy the property. It doesn't matter whether the mortgage is an "interest-only" or a "repayment" mortgage. However, it's only the interest element of the mortgage repayment that can be offset against the rental income.

EXAMPLE

Tony takes out an £80,000 interest-only mortgage to buy a rental property. His monthly repayments are £350. At the end of the year, the amount outstanding on the mortgage will still be £80,000 and the annual interest will be £4,200 (12 x £350). The entire £4,200 can be offset against his rental income.

Joan takes out an £80,000 repayment mortgage to buy a rental property. Her monthly repayments are £650. At the end of the year, the amount outstanding on her mortgage is £76,000 and, therefore, the annual interest is £3,800 (12 x £650 less the £4,000 reduction in the loan). In this case, Joan can only claim the £3,800 against her rental income.

Interest on a mortgage on your own home

You cannot deduct the interest on a loan taken out to buy your own property. However, if you later extend your mortgage and use the funds to purchase another property, then the interest on the extended portion can be offset against the rental income.

EXAMPLE

You buy an investment property for £100,000. As with many buy-to-let mortgages, you can only borrow 80% of the purchase price. Therefore, you re-mortgaged your own home to raise the additional £20,000 deposit. The interest on the £20,000 can be claimed against the rental income.

NOTE. It's unlikely your mortgage lender will give you a separate interest statement for this, so you'll need to work out the interest on the additional loan. This is done by apportioning the loan interest:

EXAMPLE

You increased your original mortgage by £20,000 to £100,000 to help buy the property and the total interest charged for the year was £6,000. The amount of interest that you can claim against your rental income is £1,200 ((£20,000/£100,000) x £6,000).

Interest on a re-mortgage

You may decide to re-mortgage the investment property (see 4.5. for more on re-mortgaging). If you re-mortgage with another lender then you can still claim the interest against your rental income. However, if you re-mortgage for a greater amount, then you can only offset the interest on the additional amount provided it doesn't exceed the value of the property when it was first let (see example 2 (Mr A) in paragraph 45700 in the HMRC's Business Income Manual (http://www.hmrc.gov.uk/manuals/bimmanual/BIM45700.htm)). If the remortgage does exceed the value of the property when first let, then you can only offset interest on the additional amount if it is used solely for the investment property (or to buy another investment property).

EXAMPLE

Nick buys a rental property for £160,000 with a mortgage of £128,000 and a monthly interest charge of £550. A few years later, the property value has increased to £200,000, so Nick decides to re-mortgage to £160,000 with monthly interest of £680. He decides to use the additional £32,000 to modernise the kitchen and bathroom in the property. Nick can therefore offset the whole of the monthly interest (£680) against his rental income.

But even if Nick had decided to use the additional £32,000 to modernise the kitchen and bathroom in his own home, then he could still offset the interest because the mortgage is still not more than the value of the property when he first brought it into his rental business. If Nick had re-mortgaged the property to £170,000 and used the additional funds for a private purpose, then he can only offset the proportion of the interest that relates to the loan on the initial value of the property (i.e. £160,000).

"Let and buy" mortgages

"Let and buy" is where you decide to buy a new home and let out your old one instead of selling it. Often, the mortgage on the existing property is increased to release funds to help buy the new one. In this case, the additional funds haven't been used on the existing property. So does this mean you can't claim the additional interest?

When you carry out this type of arrangement, you are effectively transferring the existing property to your "property investment business" at its market value on the date it is first let. You are also transferring the mortgage on the property at that date. Therefore, you can deduct all the let property mortgage interest against your rental income.

You can also deduct the additional interest where you further increase the mortgage on the let property as long as the borrowings are less than the market value of the property when it was first let.

EXAMPLE

Helen and Mark bought their original home for £80,000 with a mortgage of £70,000. Two years later, they decide to buy a new house and let their existing property that is now worth £160,000. To get the deposit for the new house, they re-mortgage to £128,000 (80%). The interest on the full £128,000 is allowable against their rental income even though they used the extra funds to purchase their own home.

Interest on personal loans

If you take out a personal loan that is used to buy, repair or improve the property, then the interest charged on this loan can be offset against rental income.

Finance agreements

If you purchase goods for your investment property using an in-store finance agreement, then the interest is an allowable expense.

NOTE. In this case, the interest can be offset whether you use the "10% wear and tear allowance" or the "renewals" method (see 2.5.).

Interest on credit cards

The interest paid on credit cards is generally not a deductible expense when calculating interest paid. This is because it's difficult to determine which part of the outstanding balance relates to funds for the property and which relates to consumer spending. However, if you originally had a nil balance on your credit card and you only use it for buying items for your property business, then there's no reason why you shouldn't claim the monthly interest charge.

TIP

Apply for a separate credit card to use solely for your property business. That way, any interest or charges paid on it will be fully deductible against your rental income.

2.2.3. How do I calculate the interest on mortgages?

At least once a year, you should receive a mortgage statement or interest certificate from your mortgage lender. This will show the amount of interest paid during the last year. If it doesn't show the interest paid to April 5, you will need to ask your lender for an up-to-date statement. Your lender may make a small charge for this (this too can be included as an expense!).

TIP

Most lenders now offer online banking. Registering for this service will allow you access to online statements, thereby avoiding the cost of requesting a paper statement showing the interest paid to April 5.

2.2.4. How do I calculate the interest on personal loans and finance agreements?

Repaying a personal loan or finance agreement usually involves making a fixed monthly payment over a set number of months. These monthly payments include both capital and interest. However, it's only the interest element of the monthly repayment that you can claim against your rental income. The problem is working out how much of each instalment you pay is interest and how much is actually paying back the loan. In fact, there are two main ways to calculate the interest element and both are acceptable to the Taxman.

Straight-line method

Using this method, the interest is calculated by dividing the total interest charges by the number of months of the loan to get a monthly interest figure.

EXAMPLE

You take out a three-year personal loan to refurbish the investment property for £15,000. The finance charges are £3,000. The total you will pay back is £18,000 so your monthly repayments are £500 (£18,000/36). Using the straight-line method, interest of £83.33 (£3,000/36) will be repaid each month.

Sum of digits method

This method takes into account the fact that you pay more interest at the beginning of a loan because there is more outstanding on it. You work out the number of payments you are going to make (e.g. for a three-year loan you will be making 36 monthly payments). You then work out the sum of digits (e.g. 1+2+3+4+5...+ 35+36 = 666 for a three year loan). The interest on the first payment is then 36/666ths of the total interest payable, the interest on the second payment is 35/666ths, the third 34/666ths and so on. The interest on the final payment is 1/666th of the total interest payable.

EXAMPLE

As above, you have taken out a £15,000 personal loan for the property over three years. The total interest payable is £3,000. The first month's interest will be £162.16 (£3000 x 36/666), the second month's £157.66 (£3000 x 35/666) and so on.

As you can see, the sum of digits method produces a much bigger interest figure to deduct against your rental income in the earlier years.

TIP

Use the sum of digits method to calculate the interest you pay on fixed-rate personal loans and finance agreements so that you can get the tax relief sooner rather than later.

2.2.5.   Plan your mortgage strategy

As a property investor, it is important for you to plan your mortgage strategy. As you can't get tax relief on a loan to buy your own property, aim to borrow as much as possible against your investment properties and use the additional funds generated to pay off the mortgage on your own property. That way, you will get tax relief on all your borrowings.

2.2.6. Mortgage arrangement fees

Fees in connection with financing of investment properties (broker's fees, arrangement fees etc.) are normally allowable against rental profits in the tax year that you incur them.

2.3. STRUCTURAL REPAIRS AND MAINTENANCE COSTS

The Taxman's general rule is that you can claim for any expenses that "prevent the property from deteriorating". This means that you can't offset the costs of any improvements you make to the property against your rental income. Due to the nature of property, the distinction between repairs and improvements is a grey area and causes many problems.

NOTE. Any improvement costs that you can't offset against your rental income can be offset against your capital gain when you sell the property (see 4.2.3.).

TIP

One of the requirements for expenditure to rank as capital improvements is that it should be relatively substantial and "one-off" in nature. So, if instead of spending a huge amount on a property all at once, you undertake a rolling programme of improvement, this is more likely to get allowed as a repair and therefore "revenue" expenditure.

2.3.1. Which structural costs can I claim?

You can claim the following costs against your rental income:

• exterior and interior painting

• damp and rot treatment

• replacing roof slates, flashing and gutters

• re-pointing

• mending broken windows

• stone cleaning.

TIP

Where you are having structural work done to a property, ask the builder for a fully itemised invoice so that you can easily identify the allowable repair costs.

2.3.2.   The exceptions

Insulation costs

The Landlord's Energy Saving Allowance (LESA) was introduced to encourage landlords to improve the energy efficiency of their residential properties. LESA allows you to claim a deduction of up to £1,500 per residential property per year for the following capital energy-saving items, provided the expenditure is incurred on or after the dates below and before April 5 2015:

- loft or cavity wall insulation from April 6 2004

- solid wall insulation from April 7 2005

- draught-proofing and insulation for hot water systems from April 6 2006

- floor insulation from April 6 2007.

This is a particularly useful relief, as, if you are renting out a property, you will have to obtain an Energy Performance Certificate for any prospective tenant which will rate the energy efficiency of your property from A to G, and your property will be more attractive to prospective tenants if you have a higher energy rating. Also, from April 2018, it will be unlawful to rent out a property which does not meet minimum energy efficiency standards and it's expected that properties will need a minimum energy rating of at least "E" to comply.

NOTE 1. You can only claim for what you actually spend, so if the costs are less than £1,500, then the maximum you can claim is what you have actually spent.

NOTE 2. The £1,500 maximum deduction is per property and not per building. This means that a maximum of £1,500 will be deductible for each flat in a block.

NOTE 3. This relief cannot be claimed where the property qualifies under the rent-a-room scheme or as furnished holiday accommodation.

Tax return. You need to enter the LESA claim in Box 35 of the UK Property pages.

Double glazing

You can claim the cost of replacing single-glazed windows with double-glazed windows against your rental income. The Taxman has agreed that this is not an improvement, but merely a replacement with the modern equivalent.

NOTE. If the Taxman accepts that double glazing is no more than the "modern equivalent" of single-glazing, then you can argue that any structural work that replaces old materials with the "modern equivalent" can be deducted from rental income. For example, the cost of replacing wooden beams with steel girders or lead pipes with copper or plastic ones would be an allowable deduction.

2.4. RENEWING FIXTURES AND FITTINGS

Fixtures and fittings are items that are attached to the property and generally cannot be removed without causing damage to it. As a rule of thumb, they are the things that are not normally removed by the seller when a property is sold. They would include:

* radiators
* light fittings
* kitchen units
* baths, washbasins and toilets.

You can claim the cost of repairing or replacing an old or broken fixture against your rental income as long as it is done on a "like-for-like" basis (i.e. with the closest modern equivalent) and not for a superior product. This is regardless of whether the property is furnished or unfurnished.

2.4.1. Can I claim the costs of a new kitchen or bathroom?

Existing let property

If you want to put a new kitchen or bathroom in a property that you've already let out, whether the costs can be reclaimed depends on whether you are just replacing "like-for-like" or making improvements too. "Like-for-like" is allowable, but improvement costs are not (http://www.hmrc.gov.uk/manuals/pimmanual/PIM2020.htm).

EXAMPLE

Fred owns and has let out a property for the past seven years. He has now decided to replace the rather worn-out bathroom suite. The original bathroom consisted of a bath, washbasin and toilet. To refurbish the bathroom and replace the old suite on a "like-for-like" basis will cost £3,000. As Fred has made no "improvements", he can claim the whole £3,000 against his rental income.

If Fred decides to add a shower (costing £500) to the bathroom when he refurbishes it, then he won't be able to claim this additional cost against his rental income. However, he will be able to claim the costs against his capital gain when he sells the property.

TIP

If you are having refurbishment work done, ask for a fully itemised invoice, so you can easily separate out the capital costs.

New property not yet let

If you've purchased a property and decide to carry out refurbishment works before you let it for the first time, it's a common misconception that you can't claim any of these costs against your rental income. This isn't always the case.

The general rule is that repairs to reinstate a dilapidated property are allowable against your rental income provided certain conditions are met. Just because you bought the property not long before the repairs were made does not in itself make the repair a capital cost.

Conditions. The main condition is whether the property was in a fit state to be let out before the repairs were carried out. If it was, then you should be able to argue that the refurbishment costs are an allowable expense against rental income. However, another factor to consider is whether the price you paid for the property was **significantly** lower as a result of the condition it was in. If it was, then the Taxman may try to argue that the repairs are capital and not deductible against your rental income.

But the repair costs will be allowable where the purchase price merely reflects the reduced value of the property due to normal wear and tear (e.g. if the previous owner had neglected to carry out routine maintenance for many years). However, do keep the receipts for any work done, because these can be offset against your capital gain when you sell the property.

> **Tip 1**
>
> If possible, consider deferring any major refurbishments until after the property is let. That way, you will be able to show the Taxman that the property was fit to be let out when purchased and, therefore, claim the costs against your rental income.

> **Tip 2**
>
> Even if you can't deduct the refurbishment costs against your rental income, still keep the receipts for any work done so that these costs can be offset against your capital gain when you sell the property.

2.5. RENEWING FURNITURE AND FURNISHINGS

Do not confuse furniture and furnishings with fixtures and fittings. Furniture and furnishings are effectively moveable items and include:

* beds

- sofas
- table and chairs
- curtains and carpets
- "white" goods such as a washing machine or freezer.

There are two ways that you can claim for the cost of renewing these items. You can either claim the actual cost of buying replacement furniture or you can claim a "wear and tear" allowance. You cannot claim both.

NOTE. Whatever method you choose, you cannot deduct the initial cost of furnishing a property against your rental income.

2.5.1. "Wear and tear" allowance

This is only relevant if the property is residential and let fully furnished. A furnished property, according to the Taxman, is one which is capable of normal occupation without the tenant having to provide their own beds, chairs, tables, sofas and other furnishings. If you provide only nominal furnishings, the property will not meet the test, and you can't claim the allowance.

TIP

Make sure you rent the property with just enough furniture to qualify as fully furnished so that you can claim the wear and tear allowance. The cost of second-hand furniture is very low compared to the tax savings you could make.

The allowance is calculated by taking 10% of the rents received after deducting any charges for services paid by you that would normally be the tenant's responsibility (e.g. water rates and Council Tax).

EXAMPLE

Martin rents out a fully furnished property for £750 a month (£9,000 a year) inclusive of water rates and Council Tax. He pays out £200 a year for water rates and £1,000 for Council Tax. He can claim a wear and tear allowance for the year of £780 (10% of (£9,000 - £1,200)). As a higher rate taxpayer, this gives him a tax saving of £312 (£780 x 40%).

The "wear and tear" allowance needs to be entered in Box 36 of the second UK Property page.

NOTE. The wear and tear allowance does not apply to furnished holiday accommodation and cannot be claimed by companies which own properties.

2.5.2. "Renewals" basis

Instead of the "wear and tear" allowance, you can claim the net cost of replacing a particular item of furniture etc. with the proviso that no relief has been claimed on the original purchase. The net cost means that you must deduct any income you receive from the sale of the old item of furniture from the purchase cost of the replacement item.

2.5.3. Which method should I use?

The wear and tear allowance is very generous and will, therefore, usually work out to be more beneficial than claiming the actual cost of replacement furniture. Also, you can start claiming the allowance as soon as you have rental income rather than wait until you replace furniture at some point in the future. However, you can only use the wear and tear allowance for fully furnished properties. Therefore, if you only partly furnish the property, then you can only use the renewals basis.

2.5.4. Can I use a different method for different properties?

Unfortunately, no. Once you have chosen a method, you have to use it on all your let furnished properties. So, if you decide to claim the wear and tear allowance, you will never be able to claim the cost of replacing furnishings and vice versa.

> **TIP**
>
> If you do own two properties and you've worked out that it's preferable to claim the wear and tear allowance for one and the renewals basis for another, then you could consider transferring one property to your spouse so that you can each claim the most beneficial method.

2.5.5. If I claim wear and tear, will I still be able to claim the cost of repairing fixtures and fittings?

Yes you can. The wear and tear rule only applies to furnishings so a claim for the cost of repairs to fixtures and fittings (see 2.4) would be allowed.

2.5.6. End of the "renewals" basis from April 2013

The Taxman has announced that, from April 1 2013 (for companies) and April 6 2013 (for individuals and partnerships), the renewals allowance will no longer be available, except for the strict statutory allowance for "trade tools" (hammer, chisel etc.) which is unlikely to be much help to property investors.

TRAP. Companies owning properties cannot claim the wear and tear allowance, so they stand to lose out when the "renewals" basis is scrapped. This is certainly something to consider when deciding whether to own your properties in a company.

TIP

If you are currently using the "renewals" basis, review the state of the furnishings in your properties and decide what will need replacing in the near future. Buy any replacements before April 2013.

2.6.   CAPITAL ALLOWANCES

As a landlord, you may have had to purchase equipment and machinery "wholly and exclusively" (see 2.1) for managing your properties. You may have bought office equipment, such as a computer, which you just use to keep your rental records. You may also own machinery for maintenance of the properties, such as a carpet washer or a drill. As these items are likely to last for more than one year, the general rule is that, you can't claim the full purchase cost against your rental income in the year you bought them but instead can claim a percentage of the cost and this percentage is known as a "capital allowance". However, there is an annual investment allowance which allows you to claim 100% of the purchase cost up to an annual limit.

NOTE. You cannot claim capital allowances on equipment or furniture inside a residential property (apart from furniture and equipment in: (i) communal areas not within any individual "dwelling" (see 2.6.2); or (ii) a furnished holiday let (see 3.2)). This is because you can claim the wear and tear allowance or the renewal cost instead (see 2.5.).

2.6.1.   How much can I claim?

The annual investment allowance for 2010/11 and 2011/12 was £100,000 but this has been reduced to £25,000 from 2012/13 onwards.

This means that for any equipment you buy after April 6 2012, you can claim 100% of the purchase cost up to a total of £25,000 (known as the annual investment allowance) for each tax year.

It is unlikely that the equipment you purchase to manage your properties will exceed the £25,000 limit for each tax year but, if it does, from April 2012 you will only be able to claim 18% (previously 20%) of the costs over the annual investment allowance against your rental profits in the tax year you buy the equipment and then 18% of the unrelieved balance of expenditure in subsequent tax years.

2.6.2. Loophole for homes of multiple occupancy (HMOs)

As we've mentioned in 2.6., you can't usually claim capital allowances for furniture and equipment in a residential property. However, there is an exception for HMOs, such as those shared by students, which are residential properties but contain communal areas, e.g. hall, stairs and landing. These areas don't count as part of the dwelling house so the equipment and furniture in them qualifies for capital allowances. Therefore, you can claim 100% of the cost (up to the annual investment allowance limit and 18% of the cost above it) of furnishings and equipment in communal areas, such as:

- carpets
- curtains
- alarm systems.

Unfortunately, a communal kitchen or lounge is considered part of the dwelling house and, therefore, you can't claim capital allowances for the equipment and furnishings in these rooms.

TIP

Even if you claim capital allowances on the furnishings in the communal areas, you can still claim the full wear and tear allowance if you let the property fully furnished. Effectively, you get a double allowance!

2.7. TRAVELLING COSTS

You can claim the cost of travelling to your investment property for:

- rent collection
- carrying out maintenance and repairs
- viewings with prospective tenants.

2.7.1. How much can I claim?

If you are travelling by car, you can either claim a proportion of the actual running costs or a fixed amount per mile.

Actual running costs

If you are using this method, then you should keep a diary of the dates and reasons you travelled to the property.

You will also need to know:

- the mileage between your home and the property (it's quite acceptable to use an internet-based route-finder to work this out)

- the total number of miles your car has done in a year (from its service record or MOT certificate)

- the annual running costs of your car (fuel, road tax, insurance, repairs and servicing).

First of all, you calculate the percentage of property business miles you have done compared with total miles for the year. You can then deduct this percentage of the running costs against your rental income. You can also deduct the same percentage of your car's capital allowance.

Most cars are not eligible for the annual investment allowance but do have their own system of capital allowances. For cars purchased before April 6 2009, the annual capital allowances from April 6 2012 onwards are the lower of:

- 18% (20% for 2011/12) of the unrelieved balance of expenditure; and

- £3,000.

For cars bought on or after April 6 2009, the capital allowances are based on the car's CO_2 emissions in the following proportions:

CO_2 EMISSIONS	CAPITAL ALLOWANCE (FROM APRIL 6 2012)
to 110g/km (reducing April 2013 to 95g/km)	100%
111 to 160g/km (reducing April 2013 to 130g/km)	18% (20% for 2011/12)
Over 160g/km (reducing April 2013 to 130g/km)	8% (10% for 2011/12)

EXAMPLE

Hugh lives in London and visits his investment property (first let in April 2012) in Leeds once a month to collect the rent and carry out any essential repairs. The journey is 200 miles each way, so he does 4,800 property business miles in a year. Hugh's total mileage for the year is 12,000 miles. Therefore, Hugh can claim 40% (4,800/12,000) of his car running costs against his rental income:

RUNNING COST	COST	40% CLAIM
Petrol	£1,700	£680
Road tax	£100	£40
Servicing	£300	£120
Insurance	£350	£140
Total	**£2,450**	**£980**

Hugh bought his car new in 2010 and its market value when he started letting his property (according to Glass's guide) was £15,000. The car has CO_2 emissions of 130g/km so the total capital allowance would therefore be 18% of this, £2,700. However, he can only claim 40% of this, i.e. £1,080. So, in total, he can deduct travelling expenses of £2,060. As a higher rate taxpayer, this will save him £824 in tax.

NOTE. The unrelieved balance of expenditure to be carried forward to the next period is calculated before the deduction for private use.

EXAMPLE

In 2013/14, the capital allowance on Hugh's car will be £2,214 ((£15,000 - £2,700) x 18%) and, assuming the private use percentage stays the same, he will be able to claim 40% of this, i.e. £885, against his rental income.

Fixed amount per mile

Rather than claiming actual costs, a much simpler method is to claim a mileage allowance. You can claim a tax-free mileage allowance of 45p per mile for the first 10,000 business miles in the tax year and then 25p after that. You still need to keep a diary of the dates and reasons you travelled to the property, but you don't have to worry about keeping a record of all the costs or calculating the capital allowance.

EXAMPLE

Taking the above example, Hugh has done 4,800 business miles. Using the 45p per mile mileage allowance, he can claim £2,160 (4,800 miles x 45p) against his rental income. In this case, he will save £864 in tax.

2.7.2.   Which method should I use?

Before the recent substantial hikes in fuel prices, it was usually much better to claim the fixed amount per mile. However, the above examples show that now there's often very little difference but it does depend on the car and the number of miles you do. Therefore, it's best to compare the two methods each year and go with the one that gives you the highest amount to claim against your rental income.

2.7.3.   How do I split the travelling expenses when I own the property with my spouse?

Joint owners can each claim their travelling expenses separately. It doesn't have to be split 50:50. It's a good idea to have the car in the name of the higher rate taxpayer so that the motoring costs can then be offset fully against their share of the rental income and get the maximum tax relief.

2.8. PRE-LETTING EXPENSES

You may have incurred expenses before letting a property. The general rule is that you can claim expenses (as long as they would qualify under normal rules, i.e. revenue expenses) incurred in the seven years before you started renting your first property. The expenses are treated as incurred on the first day that you rented a property. Examples of costs that can be claimed are:

- advertising costs incurred when searching for tenants
- telephone calls to arrange for tenants to view the property
- travel expenses incurred to show tenants around the property.

2.8.1. Can I claim the cost of mortgage interest incurred before I let the property for the first time?

As long as you are genuinely trying to let the property but it is empty because you can't find a tenant, then you can deduct the mortgage interest. Keep copies of any ads for tenants or correspondence with letting agents as evidence of this.

2.8.2. Can I deduct the cost of "doing up" the property before it's let for the first time?

As discussed in 2.4.1., the costs of any refurbishments carried out before the property is let for the first time may be allowable but it depends on whether it was in a fit state to be let out before the refurbishments were done. This is often difficult to prove to the Taxman unless the property has been let first. However, any refurbishment costs that are not allowable against your rental income can be offset against the sale proceeds to reduce your tax bill when you come to sell the property.

> TIP
>
> Make sure you keep copies of receipts for any improvements that can't be offset against your rental income so that these are not forgotten when you come to sell the property.

2.9. LEGAL AND PROFESSIONAL COSTS

You can claim all the legal and professional fees you incur in the day-to-day running of your rental business. You cannot deduct any legal fees you incur with regard to capital expenditure, e.g. buying or selling the property.

So, you can claim any fees you incur in relation to the following matters against your rental income:

- obtaining a valuation for insurance purposes

- negotiation of rent reviews

- collection of rent (debt collectors)

- property management company fees (where you use a management company to manage the rental property for you)

- evicting a tenant in order to re-let the property

- accountancy fees in preparing the letting business accounts and rental tax liability

- drawing up a new tenancy agreement that is for less than one year

- renewing a lease (as long as the lease is for less than 50 years).

Unfortunately, you can't claim the fees you incur for the following matters (although you will be able to claim them against your capital gain when you sell the property):

- purchasing or selling a property

- evicting a tenant and not intending to re-let

- architects' and surveyors' fees, etc., in improving a property

- drawing up a new tenancy agreement that is for more than one year

- planning applications (unless, for example, to carry out repairs where listed building consent is required).

2.9.1. Can I claim my accountant's fees for completing my personal tax return?

Although you can claim your accountant's fees for preparing your rental accounts, theoretically, you can't claim their fees for preparing your personal tax return. In practice, this is very rarely challenged by the Taxman. To be on the safe side, there shouldn't be any "confusing" words on your accountant's invoice i.e. it should just refer to "the completion of your rental accounts and calculation of the tax liability".

2.10. COSTS OF SERVICES PROVIDED, INCLUDING WAGES

In order to keep your rental property in good condition, you may pay for the services of a cleaner or gardener and these costs are fully allowable against your income. It is best to pay them by cheque or online banking so that you have a record of the payments. If you do pay them in cash, make sure you get some form of receipt to back up your claim.

It's absolutely fine to use the same person who cleans your own home or does your garden. However, if you pay them a total weekly amount of, say, £50, you should only claim the proportion that relates to cleaning the rented property.

2.10.1. Can I claim the cost of paying my spouse/partner a wage for managing the property?

Yes, you can pay your spouse or partner a wage for dealing with the administration of the let properties as long as they don't own part of the property. In fact, this is a good way for them to receive some income from the property without you having to give them a share in it. Their duties could include finding tenants, arranging inventories, check ins/outs, dealing with tenant queries and preparing the rental accounts etc.

2.10.2. How much can I pay them?

The Taxman says you have to pay them "a proper commercial reward" for the work they do. For a commercial rate per hour, have a look at what a managing agent would charge you and then discount this by 50% for a non-specialist putting the hours in. However, you mustn't pay less than the National Minimum Wage, currently £6.08 per hour (but rising to £6.19 per hour on October 1 2012). It's likely that a managing agent would charge a fee of at least £15 an hour, so you could pay £7.50. If you can justify just two hours work a week for 48 weeks a year, you could pay a salary of £720 for the year. As a higher rate taxpayer, this would save you £288 in tax and as long as their total income for the year (2012/13) is less than £8,105, they won't pay any tax.

NOTE. You will have to register with HMRC as an employer if one or more of the following is true:

- you are paying them at or above the NI Lower Earnings Limit which is £107 per week for 2012/13
- your spouse has another job
- they are receiving a state or other pension.

> TIP
>
> Rather than put your spouse's wages in Box 28 "Costs of services provided, including wages", put them in Box 27 "Legal, management and other professional fees" as they are "management fees for the on-going costs of letting". By doing this, you are less likely to draw the attention of the Taxman (or his computer!) and get an unnecessary enquiry.

2.11. OTHER EXPENSES

Gas safety inspection

As a landlord, you are required by law to have an annual safety inspection of all gas appliances. The inspection has to be carried out by a CORGI registered engineer who will then give you a gas safety certificate. You can claim for the cost of obtaining the certificate.

Advertising costs

If you advertise for tenants in newspapers or magazines, you can offset the costs of the ads against your rental income.

If you pay to register your property for letting on a website, you can also offset the cost against your rental income.

You cannot offset the costs of advertising your property for sale - this is a capital cost and can be offset against your capital gain (see 4.2.4.).

Magazines and books

You can offset the cost of any magazines or books for the purposes of your property business e.g. this book! Just make sure it satisfies the "wholly and exclusively" rule. For example, it may be difficult to claim for the costs of interior design magazines every month if you only redecorate a property once every five years.

Property seminar costs

Over the past few years, as the interest in property investment has increased, there has also been a steady increase in companies offering property investment seminars. Typically, these seminars cost several thousand pounds, so it would be nice to be able to deduct them from your rental income.

If you're already a property investor and attend a course to refresh your investment skills, then you can offset the entire cost, as you will be regarded as updating your skills.

However, if you're thinking of investing in property for the first time and attend a course to explain how to do this, then you will not be able to offset the costs against the rental income. This is because you will not just be "updating your skills", you will be learning new ones.

TAXMAN WARNING! Having large seminar costs in Box 29 "Other allowable property expenses" could trigger an investigation. If you have had an investment business for a few years and are just updating your knowledge, then include the breakdown of other expenses in the white space on your tax return.

Telephone and Internet

You can claim the cost of any telephone calls you make with regard to your property business such as those to a letting agent or tenant. Strictly, you should keep a log of these calls, but, in practice, a reasonable estimate of the split between private and business use will usually be acceptable. You can also claim a suitable proportion of the line rental and Internet charges.

TIP

Check whether your phone company allows you to split your telephone bill into two sections by entering a code before dialling the number. That way you can have one code for property business calls and another for personal calls and they will be shown separately on the bill.

Use of home as office

Like most property investors, you probably manage your let properties from home. So, can you claim part of the general running costs of your home against your rental income? Well, you might have thought that because expenses must be incurred "wholly and exclusively" you wouldn't get any relief. However, in practice, the Taxman agrees that where there is part-business and part-private use of a home, the running costs can be apportioned.

If you do have a separate study/office to run your property business, then you can claim a share of your home running costs based on the proportion of the room in relation to your whole house. This is supposed to be done on a "floor area" basis, but in practice, the Taxman allows a proportion based on the number of rooms in a house (excluding bathrooms, toilets, kitchens, landings and hallways). For example, if you have five bedrooms and three reception rooms in your house and one of them is dedicated to your property business, then you can deduct 1/8th of your running costs. Allowable running costs include Council Tax (or rates), water rates, mortgage interest, general repairs to the fabric of the building, and buildings and contents insurance. Heating and lighting costs can be apportioned on the same basis, though it may be that the facts support apportioning a larger amount to the office on the basis of usage. After all, the computer is on all day. And if an office or study has been built specifically for the business, there is no reason why interest on any loan taken out to finance the building work should not be deductible in full.

NOTE. Using the "number of rooms" allocation method is not compulsory and you can use any method that produces a reasonable result.

However, if "working from home" involves little more than setting papers out on a corner of the dining-room table for a few hours a month, then you may find it hard to convince the Taxman that you've incurred additional costs.

TIP

Small claims not exceeding £4 per week (£3 per week for 2011/12) should be acceptable even for very minimal business use as these are the rates that the Taxman allows employees to claim for working from home without the need to justify the expenses.

If your spare bedroom doubles as an office during the week and guest accommodation at the weekend then you need to apportion the total running costs first on the basis of floor area (or number of rooms). The part relating to the room should then be apportioned by reference to the time it is used for domestic or rental business purposes e.g. 5/7ths.

TAXMAN WARNING! If you use a room in your own home exclusively for business, then the Taxman may disallow a proportion of the principal private residence relief (see 5.1) when you come to sell the property. The way round this is simply to make sure that the room is used for both private and business purposes and the expenses claim calculation reflects this.

3. Making the most of your rental losses

3.1. WHAT IS A RENTAL LOSS?

You will incur a rental loss if the expenses you claim against your rental income are greater than the rent you receive. The treatment of losses is different depending on whether you have general UK property, furnished holiday accommodation (see 3.2.) or overseas property. Losses on overseas property will be dealt with in 12.2.5.

3.1.1. What can I do with a loss on general UK property?

More than one property

If you have several properties, then any loss you make on one is automatically set off against the profits from the others, in the same year. This is because the income from all your UK properties (except furnished holiday accommodation) is treated as a single property "business" (see 1.2.2.).

Overall net loss

If the rental profits from other properties don't cover the whole loss, or you don't own any other properties, then you can carry the loss forward and set it against your rental income of the following tax years until it is used up.

EXAMPLE

In the tax year ending April 5 2013, Angie received rental income of £5,000. However, her total property expenses were £6,000, so she made a £1,000 loss and had no tax to pay. In the following tax year to April 5 2014, Angie receives rent of £6,000 and pays out £4,000 in expenses. Therefore, she has made a profit of £2,000. But Angie can offset the previous year's loss of £1,000 against this. So, although she's made a profit of £2,000, she's only taxed on £1,000 of it.

3.1.2. How do I claim the loss?

You don't need to write a separate letter to the Taxman to claim the loss. On the second "UK Property" page, enter the amount of the loss to carry forward in Box 43 "Loss to carry forward to following year".

3.1.3. Can I offset losses from a previous UK property against income from one bought several years later?

If you stop investing in property for several years and then start again, you could be classed as ceasing one business and starting up another. Therefore, theoretically, the rental losses would disappear when the first source of rental income stops.

<u>What was your intention?</u>

However, if it was your intention when selling the old investment property to purchase another one and let it out, then even though you didn't do so until several years later, you have a strong argument (backed up by case law - Kirk & Randall Ltd v Dunn) for carrying the loss forward and setting it off against the profits arising on the new property. As always, the challenge is in convincing the Taxman that it was your intention. Therefore, to strengthen your case, make sure you keep a record of all the potential investment properties you looked at prior to buying the second property (take pictures), correspondence with estate agents and dates you visited property auctions etc.

TIP 1

To help show it was your intention not to cease the property business, ensure that any cash received on the sale of the previous UK property is not used in another business or for a personal purpose, such as buying your own home.

TIP 2

Box 2 of the "UK Property" pages asks you to put in an "X" if you don't expect to receive rental income in the following tax year. You would be best to leave this box blank if you have property losses that you wish to offset in the future otherwise the Taxman may try to use it as a strong indicator that your property business has ceased.

NOTE. As long as you still have at least one UK property let out on a commercial basis, you still have a property business that you can offset losses from previous properties against.

3.1.4. Can I offset the loss against my other income in the year?

Generally, no. Although rental profits and losses are calculated in much the same way as self-employed businesses, the treatment of losses is different.

Unlike self-employed business losses, rental losses cannot be offset against the other income of the taxpayer. However, there are two notable exceptions: losses on furnished holiday accommodation (see 3.2) and excess capital allowances.

Exception - excess capital allowances claimed

As discussed in 2.6., if you let residential property, you can claim "capital allowances" for certain equipment you use in your property business (as long as it's not kept inside the let property). If you own and let out commercial property (including furnished holiday accommodation) then you have even more opportunity to claim capital allowances (see 9.5.).

So, if you have claimed capital allowances against your rental income in calculating the loss, then you can make a claim to offset these capital allowances against your other income in the year of the loss (or the following year) instead. The advantage of this is that you will get tax relief for part of the loss now, rather than in some future tax year. The capital allowances you offset must not exceed your rental loss.

EXAMPLE

Frank makes a rental loss of £1,000 in the year ended April 5 2013. Included in his property expenses are capital allowances of £900 relating to equipment he bought to run his letting business.

Frank can make a claim to offset the £900 capital allowances against his other income in the year to April 5 2013. The remaining £100 of the loss will be carried forward and set against future profits from his letting business. If Frank is a higher-rate taxpayer, he will make a tax saving in 2012/13 of £360.

If Frank's capital allowances had been £1,100, he could only have offset a maximum of £1,000 against his other income as he can't offset more than the loss.

To make the claim, enter the amount of the capital allowances in Box 42 on the "UK Property" pages. This claim must be made within twelve months of the January 31 filing deadline. So, a claim for the year ended April 5 2013 would have to be made by January 31 2015. This means that even if you've already submitted your tax return, you can make a claim to change it by sending the Taxman amended "UK Property" pages with Box 42 completed.

3.1.5. Can I let a property to a relative for a nominal rent and still claim all my property related expenses?

Yes, you can. The only problem is that as the letting is not on a "commercial" basis, the Taxman will not allow you to offset the loss against the rental profits of any other properties.

In fact, all you can do with the loss is carry it forward and offset it against any future profits you make on the same letting (i.e. the same tenant at the same property). Therefore, there's no real tax advantage in making a loss on a non-commercially let property.

3.1.6. If I always make losses on my rental property, do I need to declare them to the Taxman?

As mentioned in 1.3.2., in theory, you should let the Taxman know that you have a new source of income by October 5 of the following tax year. However, in practice, as long as you complete a tax return by January 31 of the following year showing the new source of income, you won't incur a penalty.

Obviously, the Taxman won't necessarily find out if you don't tell him about your new source of income. However, if you don't declare the losses and then you begin to make profits in later years, you won't be able to offset any of these losses against the future profits. Therefore, you may end up paying more tax than you would if you had declared the losses in the first place.

3.2. FURNISHED HOLIDAY HOMES

Letting property is treated as a business; however, it is not treated as a "trade". This means that your net rental income is not considered "earned" income. However, there is an exception. If you invest in and let a UK property that qualifies as a "furnished holiday home", then it will be treated as "earned" income and will therefore benefit from some attractive income tax rules:

- your net income from holiday lets counts as part of your earnings for pension contributions

- you can claim capital allowances on any money spent on furnishings and equipment for the holiday home (this isn't available to most residential accommodation - see 2.6.)

- up until April 5 2011, if you made a loss on your holiday let(s), you could offset it against your other income in the year (see 3.2.3.) and claim a tax rebate. There is no relief against general income for losses arising from any other kind of letting. However, this relief was abolished from the 2011/12 tax year onwards.

NOTE. Although it is treated as earned income, there's no need to pay Class 4 National Insurance contributions.

There are also significant Capital Gains Tax advantages which are discussed in 6.2.

3.2.1. Does my property qualify as a "furnished holiday home"?

With such appealing tax advantages on offer, you won't be surprised to learn that there are strict qualifying criteria which were further increased for 2012/13 onwards:

- the accommodation must be furnished (to at least the minimum level which an occupier would usually expect); and

- it must be available for commercial letting (see 3.2.2.) to the public generally (i.e. not your family!), as furnished holiday accommodation, for at least 210 days (30 weeks) a year (previously 140 days); and

- it must actually be let for at least 105 days (15 weeks) a year (previously 70 days); and

- in any period of at least seven months, the property should not normally be let to the same person for more than a month (technically 31 days) at a time; and

- the property must be situated in the UK or European Economic Area (EEA).

NOTE 1. If you've let more than one furnished holiday home, then you don't have to let out both properties for 105 days each as long as the average is 105 days or more. So, if you had two properties, one could be let for 95 days and the other for 115 days.

NOTE 2. From 2010/11 onwards, you can elect for a property which qualified as a furnished holiday home under the above criteria in the previous tax year to continue to qualify as a furnished holiday home for up to two further tax years even if it wasn't let for 105 days in those two tax years. In other words, a property only needs to be let for 105 days in a year once in every three years. The property will still need to meet all the other criteria.

TIP

Make sure you keep your booking diary showing the names and addresses of the holidaymakers together with the dates of their stay. This will provide proof to the Taxman, if required.

3.2.2. What does the Taxman view as "commercial letting"?

As the reliefs for qualifying holiday lets are so generous, the Taxman will look very closely at them. In particular, he will want to see that you have set up the holiday letting business in order to make profits. Therefore, if your main motive is to buy a second home (perhaps for retirement), then the Taxman may disallow it as a holiday home even though you fulfil the other criteria. Also, the letting is very unlikely to qualify if the interest on any loan you take out to buy the property is always more than the rental income.

This doesn't mean you're expected to make a profit on your holiday home from day one, but the Taxman would expect to see the holiday home business being profitable within five years of starting.

TIP

In order to establish, if need be at a later date, that the letting is on a "commercial" basis, produce a spreadsheet showing the income you expect to be generated from it over the next five years and the related expenses (which must be less!). In particular, make sure the annual mortgage interest is less than the expected rental income.

3.2.3. What can I do with a loss on furnished holiday accommodation?

Offset against other income?

As mentioned in 3.2., up until April 5 2011, if you made a loss on your holiday let, you could offset it against your other income either in the tax year of the loss or the year before. However, from 2011/12 onwards, this relief was abolished meaning that losses can only be carried forward and offset against future profits from the same furnished holiday letting business.

Carry forward

As mentioned above, from 2011/12 onwards, if you make a loss on your furnished holiday lets, then all you can do is carry it forward and offset it against the first available future profits you make on the same holiday letting business.

NOTE. All of your UK holiday lets are regarded as one business, with all holiday lets outside of the UK, but in the EEA, regarded as a separate business.

TIP

See Appendix A for a list of countries within the EEA.

Avoiding tax on rental income

SECTION II

Avoiding tax on property disposals

4. Capital gains - the tax basics

4.1. WHAT IS CAPITAL GAINS TAX?

At some point in the future, it's likely that you will want to sell your investment property. If you're resident in the UK for tax purposes, Capital Gains Tax (CGT) is the tax that you have to pay on any capital gain (essentially the difference between what you paid for it and what you sold it for) you make on the sale. So, if your investment property has increased in value, it's likely you will have a taxable capital gain. If you're a higher rate taxpayer, this could reduce your investment by up to 40%.

Substantial changes to the taxation of capital gains came into effect on June 23 2010 and this chapter explains the rules for properties after that date.

NOTE. Remember it is the date of exchange of contracts that is treated as the date of sale and not the completion date.

4.1.1. Do I have to pay CGT?

If you are resident, ordinarily resident, and domiciled in the UK, you will be liable to CGT on the sale of your worldwide property.

Non-UK residents are generally exempt from CGT.

If you are UK resident, but either not ordinarily resident or not UK domiciled, then you will still be liable to CGT on the sale of your UK property but you can opt to only be liable for CGT on your overseas property sales if and when you remit the proceeds back to the UK. However, to take advantage of this you will have to pay a remittance charge which, from April 2012, is £50,000 if you have been resident in the UK for twelve out of the last 14 years.

Companies do not pay CGT, but instead pay Corporation Tax on their capital gains.

NOTE. The government is proposing to introduce a Statutory Residence Test (SRT) which will come into effect in April 2013. This SRT will effectively make the concept of ordinary residence redundant and it will be abolished. The details have not been finalised but it is likely that a series of tests will be introduced which will enable an individual to arrive at a definitive answer to the question *"Am I resident in the UK?"*

4.1.2. What's the rate of CGT?

For capital gains made on disposals from June 23 2010, CGT is paid at two main rates:

- 18% on gains made by basic rate taxpayers

- 28% on gains made by higher and additional rate taxpayers.

Therefore, for 2012/13, an individual will pay 28% tax on their capital gains to the extent that their total taxable income for the year (after deducting the personal allowance) plus their total taxable capital gains exceeds the £34,370 (the higher rate threshold).

Trusts pay CGT at only one rate - 28%.

> **TIP**
>
> As the rate of CGT depends on your total income, you may be able to reduce your CGT bill by ensuring that your gains fall into a year when you have less other income.

4.1.3. Can I avoid CGT by just giving the property away?

Unfortunately, as a general rule, no! If you decide to transfer or gift your property to someone else, then you will be deemed to have sold the property at the market value on the date of the gift. This means that you could end up with a tax bill even though you haven't received any sale proceeds. However, there are ways of getting around this rule and avoiding CGT when transferring or gifting certain property - see Chapter 6.

4.1.4. Are there special rules for spouses and civil partners?

Yes. For CGT purposes, spouses are treated as one person. If you transfer a property to your spouse or civil partner, there is no CGT to pay. However, if your spouse eventually sells the property, the capital gain will be calculated based on the original cost and not the value when the property was transferred.

4.1.5. How much is the annual CGT allowance?

For 2012/13, each individual has an annual CGT exemption of £10,600. This means that you won't pay any CGT unless your total taxable gains in a tax year are more than £10,600.

EXAMPLE

Lynn, a higher rate taxpayer, has made a taxable gain of £50,000 on her investment property. She has no other gains for the year, so she can reduce this gain by the £10,600 annual exemption. She will, therefore, pay tax on only £39,400 of the gain.

TIP

A husband and wife (or civil partners) each get their own separate exemption, so transfer the property into joint names with your spouse to double your tax-free gains to £21,200 and save additional tax of up to £2,968. See 7.2. to find out how transfer part of the property to your spouse.

NOTE. If you have no other income in the year, then the maximum exemption is still £10,600, i.e. you can't offset the £8,105 income tax personal allowance as well.

4.1.6. Which tax returns do I need to complete for capital gains?

You need to complete the "Capital gains summary" supplementary pages for the tax year (April 6 to April 5) in which you made the gain if:

- the proceeds are more than four times the annual exemption (i.e. more than £42,400 for 2012/13) or
- CGT is due on the gain.

As it's likely that you will sell your property for more than £42,400, you will need to complete the "Capital gains summary" pages whether you have to pay CGT on the gain or not. The only exception is where the gain is completely covered by the Principal Private Residence exemption (see 5.1.).

So if you made a gain in July 2012, you will need to include the "Capital gains summary" pages in your 2012/13 tax return, which needs to be submitted to the Taxman by January 31 2014.

If you have been sent a paper tax return without these supplementary pages, you can download them from the Taxman's website at http://www.hmrc.gov.uk/forms/sa108.pdf.

4.1.7. When do I have to pay the tax?

As the capital gains are shown on your self-assessment tax return, you need to pay the tax by January 31 following the tax year. So, the tax on gains in the year to April 5 2013 has to be paid by January 31 2014.

4.1.8. What's the date of sale; when we exchange contracts or when we complete?

For CGT purposes, the date of disposal is the date of the contract. Therefore, it's normally the date of exchange and not the date of completion. This is extremely important when a sale takes place around April 5.

EXAMPLE

Pauline exchanges contracts on March 21 2013 but completion doesn't take place until April 10 2013. Pauline mistakenly thinks that she can claim that the sale took place in the tax year 2013/14, so that the tax isn't payable until January 31 2015, 21 months later. This is entirely wrong. The sale actually took place on March 21 2013 in the tax year 2012/13, meaning that the tax is due by January 31 2014, only ten months later. If the Taxman discovers the error, Pauline will be charged interest from the date when the tax should have been paid. She may also incur penalties.

TIP

If you want to delay the paying of the CGT by twelve months, ask your solicitor to delay the exchange of contracts until after April 5. That way, the gain will fall into the following tax year so any tax payable is due by January 31 a year later.

4.1.9. How do I calculate the capital gain?

This is not particularly straightforward, but simply, the capital gain is calculated by taking the selling price and deducting (in the following order):

* allowable costs (see 4.2.)
* any other relevant reliefs (such as principal private residence relief)
* allowable losses (see 4.6.)
* the annual exemption (see 4.1.5.).

Download Zone

For an interactive calculator, visit **http://books.indicator.co.uk**. You'll find the access code on page 2 of this book.

4.2. REDUCE THE GAIN BY CLAIMING ALL ALLOWABLE COSTS

When working out the gain, the first thing to do is add up all the costs you incurred during the purchase and sale of the property. Then, add the purchase costs to the basic buying price and deduct the selling costs from the sale price. The idea is to maximise the purchase price and minimise the selling price so that the difference between the two (i.e. your gain) is reduced as much as possible.

4.2.1. Buying costs

Add onto your purchase price any costs that you incurred in order to buy the property. Typical costs include:

- survey fees
- solicitors' fees and searches
- Stamp Duty Land Tax.

NOTE. As a rule of thumb, all the costs on the completion statement from your solicitor will be allowable (so make sure you keep a copy with your tax documents).

4.2.2. Travelling expenses

Your property may not be near where you live. In this case, you can quite legitimately claim the costs you may have originally incurred in dealing with the property purchase such as viewing the property and meetings with solicitors, surveyors etc.

Remember not to include the costs of visiting the property to collect rent or carry out repairs, as these costs should be offset against your rental income (see 2.7.). Again, add these travel costs onto your purchase price.

TIP

Rather than claiming actual costs, a much simpler method is to claim a mileage allowance. You can claim a tax-free mileage allowance of 45p for the first 10,000 business miles and then 25p after that. Keep a diary of the dates you travelled to the various prospective properties just in case the Taxman queries your claim.

4.2.3. Enhancement costs

If you previously let the property, then you weren't able to offset the costs of any improvements (i.e. capital costs) against your rental income (see 2.3.). However, you can deduct these costs from the sale proceeds as long as the enhancements are still there when you sell the property, i.e. they are permanent improvements.

For example, you can claim the cost of adding a conservatory, loft extension or improving the kitchen. So, always keep the receipts for any improvement work you've had done.

TIP

If you couldn't offset the costs against your rental income then you will usually be able to offset them against your capital gain when you sell the property. When your annual rental accounts are prepared, keep a list of all disallowed expenditure. This list can then be reviewed when you sell the property, so that no items of expenditure are missed.

4.2.4. Selling costs

Deduct any costs incurred when selling the property from your selling price. Such costs include:

- solicitors' fees

- advertising costs

- estate agent's commission

- travelling costs - associated with selling the property such as being there for viewings with potential buyers or meeting with local estate agents. Again, you can claim 45p per mile for the first 10,000 miles and 25p thereafter.

4.2.5. Can I deduct the mortgage early redemption penalty?

Unfortunately, if you are redeeming a mortgage early, you can't deduct any early redemption penalty from your selling price. But you should be able to offset it against any rental income in the tax year. The Taxman's guidance (http://www. hmrc.gov.uk/manuals/bimmanual/bim45820.htm) states that:

"The majority of break payments that take the form of a penalty for early redemption of the loan will represent bona fide compensation to the lender. In such circumstances the break payment will not amount to a premium and will therefore attract relief as "incidental costs of raising loan finance"."

4.3. CGT-AVOIDANCE STRATEGY - DON'T SELL, JUST REMORTGAGE

Over the years, your property has risen significantly in value. Rather than sell the property (and trigger a large CGT bill), you could realise the "profit" by re-mortgaging and getting some cash out of the investment.

4.3.1. What are the short-term benefits?

If you sell a property, you will have to pay tax on any gain you make. However, if you re-mortgage the property, you have not actually made a disposal as you still own the property so there is no tax to pay on the capital you take out.

EXAMPLE

Steve, a higher rate taxpayer, has an investment property in Kent which has significantly increased in value since he bought it for £40,000 in April 2000. It was recently valued at £200,000. Steve feels that the property values in Kent have levelled off, and he is now looking to invest in a new city centre development in Bristol.

In order to buy the Bristol property, Steve needs to release some of the cash tied up in his Kent property. If he sells the Kent property, he would be looking at a CGT bill of £41,832 ((£200,000 - £40,000 - £10,600) x 28%). After repaying his 90% mortgage (£36,000) on his Kent property, Steve would have £122,168 to invest in Bristol.

Instead of selling, Steve decides to re-mortgage the Kent property. The new mortgage is for 80% of the current value, £160,000. Therefore, after paying off his original mortgage, Steve has £124,000. So he now has £1,832 more to invest in Bristol than if he had sold the property even before taking into account selling costs such as estate agents' commission and solicitors' fees. He also still has £40,000 equity in the Kent property and an income-producing asset.

SELL. You have made a disposal and there will be tax to pay on any gain.

RE-MORTGAGE. You have not made a disposal and still own the property so there is no tax on the capital you take out.

4.3.2. Long-term trap

CGT is based on the difference between sale proceeds and purchase cost. In order to calculate the capital gain when you sell a property, you deduct the original cost of the property and not the outstanding mortgage amount from your sale proceeds. However, where you've re-mortgaged and spent the additional funds on other properties, you could find that the "equity" left in the property is not enough to cover your CGT bill:

EXAMPLE

After one year, Steve's property in Kent is proving difficult to rent so he decides to sell. As he suspected, the property value has levelled off so he sells for £200,000. The balance on the interest-only mortgage is £160,000 and he has selling costs of £4,000. His CGT bill is therefore £40,712. Therefore, after tax, he still has to find an extra £4,712 to settle the tax bill.

Avoiding tax on property disposals

II

TIP

Avoid getting into this situation by limiting the amount you re-mortgage by. The rule of thumb is to limit your borrowing to a maximum cost of "original cost plus 70% of any increase in value".

EXAMPLE

If Steve had limited his borrowing using the above formula, he would have re-mortgaged to a maximum of £40,000 plus 70% of the increase in value, £112,000 (160,000 x 70%). This works out as £152,000. By doing this, he could have paid the CGT bill and selling costs and still had £3,288 left over.

Download Zone

For our interactive calculator, visit **http://books.indicator.co.uk**. You'll find the access code on page 2 of the book.

NOTE. If you are using the funds to make improvements to the re-mortgaged property, then the cost of these improvements needs to be added to the original cost to work out the maximum that can be re-mortgaged.

4.4. ALLOWABLE LOSSES

You can offset any losses you make from the sale of one property against the gain on another. If you don't have any such gains, then the loss can be carried forward and set off against the first available gains in future years. If losses are carried forward, they can only be offset to the extent necessary to reduce the future gains down to the annual exemption applying for that future year.

TIP

You are free to allocate your annual exemption and any capital losses you have available in the most beneficial manner. This is unlikely to have much impact unless you have any gains which are eligible for entrepreneurs' relief (taxed at only 10%), for example from the sale of furnished holiday lets, and gains which are not. In this case, you should allocate the annual exemption and any capital losses to the gains which are not eligible for entrepreneurs' relief.

4.5. CGT-AVOIDANCE STRATEGY - OFFSET STOCK MARKET LOSSES AGAINST YOUR PROPERTY GAIN

CGT isn't just due on gains on the sale of properties. It is also due, for example, on any gain made on the sale of shares or unit trusts. The advantage of this is that if you have made losses on shares, (which is not uncommon given the recent stock market falls), then you can offset this loss against any gain you make on the sale of your property.

EXAMPLE

In the late 1990s, George invested £10,000 in dot.com shares, but subsequently sold them in 2008 for just £100. George also had an investment property that he sold in 2008, making a taxable gain of £18,000. George can reduce the gain on the sale of his investment property to £8,100 by offsetting his £9,900 share loss. As George's gain is now less than his annual allowance, he ends up with no tax to pay.

4.5.1. Can I offset stock market losses from previous years?

Yes, you can. However, you need to have shown these losses on your tax return in the tax year that they occurred i.e. the year that you sold the shares.

NOTE. You only make a loss (for CGT purposes) when you actually sell the shares. Therefore, you can't normally offset any loss you've made "on paper" if you still own the shares (see 4.5.2. for the exception).

TIP

If you hadn't originally included the losses on your tax return in the year that they were made, then you can still claim the losses up to four years from the end of the relevant tax year. So if, for example, you made losses in 2008/9, you have until April 5 2013 to claim them. See Appendix B for a sample claim letter.

4.5.2. Do I actually have to sell the shares to claim the loss?

Usually, yes. However, the situation is different if the Taxman agrees that the quoted shares are effectively worthless (check the Taxman's negligible value list at http://www.hmrc.gov.uk/cgt/negvalist.htm).

If the shares are included on his list, then you can make a claim for the shares to be treated as though you sold them on the date you made the claim or up to two years before the tax year in which you make the claim (as long as they were worthless at the time). You can, therefore, make a loss without actually selling the shares.

TIP

You can make a negligible value claim at any time after the shares have become worthless. Therefore, defer a claim until there are sufficient gains to avoid you wasting your annual exemption (£10,600 for 2012/13).

See Appendix C for a sample negligible value claim letter.

5. Avoid CGT by using "principal private residence" relief

5.1. PRINCIPAL PRIVATE RESIDENCE RELIEF (PPR)

5.1.1. What is "principal private residence" relief?

You are probably aware that when you sell your own home, you don't have to pay tax on any gain you make. This is known as "principal private residence" relief (PPR relief). However, as a property investor, you can use this relief to your advantage and make substantial CGT savings (often wiping out the gain completely).

5.1.2. Is it available to me?

This relief is available to you if the property has, at some time, been classed as your only or main residence.

5.1.3. How much can I claim?

This depends on whether you qualify for full or partial relief:

Full relief

If the property was your only or main home throughout your period of ownership (excluding the last three years, see 5.1.4.), then you can automatically claim full PPR relief so you have no CGT liability. This is regardless of the "capital gain" you make on the property.

> EXAMPLE
>
> Kitty buys her first home in June 1992 for £48,000. She lives in it from the date of purchase up until the day she sells it in June 2001 for £120,000. Kitty has made a capital gain of £72,000, but she pays no CGT. She can claim full residence relief because the property was her main residence throughout her period of ownership.

Partial relief

If the property was your main home for only part of your period of ownership, then the amount of relief you can claim is calculated by dividing the period(s) when the property was your PPR (including the last three years of ownership (see 5.1.4) and certain other periods of absence (see 5.1.5.)) by the total length of time you owned the property.

EXAMPLE

Harry buys a home in April 1993 for £50,000. He lives there until June 1995 before moving to a bigger home nearby. Harry eventually sells his original house in May 2003 for £120,000. The house was Harry's main residence for 26 months and he owned the property for a total of 121 months. Therefore, the house is treated as being Harry's PPR for 62 months (the 26 months he actually lived there plus the last 36 months) and the amount of relief he can claim is 62/121ths of £70,000. His taxable gain is £34,132.

NOTE. When calculating this relief, ignore any periods of ownership before March 31 1982.

5.1.4. The "three-year rule"

As long as the property was your main residence at some point, the last three years of ownership will also always qualify for the relief.

NOTE. If you lived in the property at any time during the last three years of ownership, you can't make a claim for the additional three years as well.

EXAMPLE

Taking the first example in 5.1.3.; Kitty moves in with her partner in June 1998 and lets her original property. In this case, when she sells the property in June 2001, she can still claim maximum PPR relief. This is because the property was her main residence for six out of the nine years she owned it and, because it used to be her main residence, she is entitled to the bonus of the last three years.

TIP

Sell the property within three years of it being your main residence and avoid paying any CGT.

The "three-year rule" also means you can effectively claim double PPR - on the last three years of your old property and on your new property at the same time.

5.1.5. Which other periods of absence from the property still qualify for PPR relief?

In addition to the periods when the property was actually your main residence, you can also include certain periods when you were absent from the property in order to work out the length of time it was your PPR.

NOTE. For these periods to qualify as periods of occupation, the property must actually be your main residence both before and after these absences. Also, while you're away, you can't have a different main residence.

The periods of absence that count towards PPR relief are:

* three years for any reason whatsoever (it can be a single period of three years or shorter periods as long as they don't add up to more than three years in total)

* a period of up to four years when you (or your spouse) are required to work elsewhere in the UK as part of your job

* a period of any length when you (or your spouse) are required to work abroad. You will keep the exemption for these absences even if you are unable to return to the property afterwards because you are required to work elsewhere on your return.

Therefore, you can have long periods of absence from the property without losing any part of your PPR exemption.

EXAMPLE

Nick buys a home in Bournemouth in February 1993 and lived in it as his only residence. In October 1993, his employer required him to work in Reading. He lived there in a flat provided by his employer until October 1998. Then his employer transferred him to work in Melbourne and also provided a flat there. He ended his employment in March 2000 and toured Europe until November 2000. Then he returned to his home in Bournemouth and stayed there until he sold it in February 2004. The whole of the period of ownership qualifies for PPR relief:

February 1993 - October 1993 - only or main residence October 1993 - October 1997 - four years absence as required to work elsewhere in UK October 1997 - October 1998 - one year of absence for any reason October 1998 - March 2000 - period of absence due to employment abroad March 2000 - November 2000 - seven months absence for whatever reason November 2000 - February 2004 - only or main residence.

You can apply the rules in any way that is most beneficial to you. For example, if the period from October 1993 - October 1997 had been treated as part of the "three years for any reason" that would have used up the three year allowance and so no relief would have been available for the period between March and November 2000.

5.1.6. What happens if I've bought a property, but can't move in until it's done up?

You may not be able to move into your new property straightaway because it's still being built, needs refurbishing or you're having trouble selling your old property. However, you can still treat the new property as your PPR from the date you bought it as long as you move in within twelve months (this won't affect the PPR status of your old property because of the "three year rule"). And if you can't move in due to reasons beyond your control, you can even extend this period to two years.

5.1.7. If I move into my property after I've let it out for a few years, can I still claim PPR relief?

Yes, you can. You do not need to live in the property first in order to claim partial PPR relief for the time it was your main residence.

5.2. PRIVATE LETTING RELIEF

5.2.1. Is it available to me?

If you let out your main residence (all or part of it) as residential (not commercial) accommodation, then you can claim "private letting relief". It makes no difference whether you let the property out before or after it became your main residence.

5.2.2. What's it worth?

The amount of private letting relief that you can claim is the lower of:

• the amount of PPR relief

• £40,000

• the gain before letting relief is set-off (i.e. this relief cannot create a capital loss).

Therefore, if the amount of the gain covered by PPR relief is less than £40,000, then the letting relief can never be more than the PPR relief.

EXAMPLE

David bought a house in June 2006 for £100,000 and lived in it as his main residence for one year. He then moved out and let the property for five years before selling it in June 2013 for £240,000. David can claim PPR relief for 48 months (the twelve months he lived there plus the last three years) of the 72 months he owned the property. Therefore, £46,667 of the gain is potentially taxable.

However, David can claim maximum private letting relief of £40,000 (the PPR relief is £100,000), reducing his gain to just £6,667. He can then offset the annual exemption of £10,600 so he ends up with no tax to pay. By living in the property for just one year, David has made a tax-free gain of £140,000, a tax saving of £25,200.

5.2.3. Can a husband and wife or registered civil partners each claim the relief?

Yes! Where the property is jointly owned and jointly let by the husband and wife, each may be entitled to the £40,000 maximum relief. This makes the relief potentially very valuable.

5.3. CGT-AVOIDANCE STRATEGY: "LIVE AND LET" NOT "BUY-TO-LET"

Problem

If you invest in a buy-to-let property, let it and then sell it, it will never have been your main residence. If the property has never been your home then you miss out on claiming both PPR relief and private letting relief on any capital gain you make.

Solution

Instead of investing in a buy-to-let property, let out the house that has been your main residence and move into a new property.

Tax advantage

As the let property was once your main residence, the last three years of ownership are exempt from CGT (see 5.1.4.). So, if you sell the property within three years then you automatically have no tax to pay. If the property is sold after more than three years, then private letting relief can reduce (or even eradicate) the capital gain.

EXAMPLE

Kate bought her property in 1992 for £48,000 and lived there until she moved in with her partner in June 1998. She let her original property for five years before selling it in June 2003 for £150,000. The first six years of ownership are exempt from CGT as it was her main residence. The last three years of ownership are also exempt (remember the "three year rule") because the property used to be her main residence. That leaves a potential gain of £18,545 (2/11ths of £102,000).

However, this gain is wiped out by private letting relief (the gain is less than £40,000) because the property used to be Kate's main residence and was then let out. So Kate has made a tax-free gain of £102,000.

Rule of thumb

You can make a CGT-free gain on your property of up to £80,000 as long as you sell the let property within 2 x (n + 3) years, where n is the number of years the property was actually your main residence (i.e. don't count the last three years of ownership).

5.4.   CGT-AVOIDANCE STRATEGY: "LET AND LIVE"

Problem

You already own an investment property that you have let out for a number of years. You have never lived in the property so will be unable to claim both PPR and private letting relief. Therefore, you are facing a hefty CGT bill when you sell the property.

Solution

Make sure you live in the previously let property before you sell it.

Tax advantage

By making the property your main residence for only a short time, not only can you claim PPR relief, but you can also claim private letting relief too.

EXAMPLE

Adam buys a property in September 2006 for £40,000 and rents it out for four years. He then lives in it for one year and sells it in September 2012 for £120,000. As the property was his main residence, the last three years are exempt (remember the "three year rule"). Therefore, the PPR relief is £48,000 (3/5ths £80,000). This leaves a gain of £32,000 which, being less than £40,000, can be completely eradicated by private letting relief. As a higher rate taxpayer, by living in the property for just one year, Adam has saved £19,432 in tax (28% x £80,000 - £10,600).

TAXMAN WARNING! If you decide to use this strategy on a regular basis, then the Taxman will look closely to see if the property was actually your main residence.

5.4.1.   Is there a minimum length of time that I have to live in the property to claim PPR relief?

The Taxman hasn't issued any specific guidance on this, but obviously, the longer you live in the property, the better chance you have of claiming PPR relief.

However, the Taxman is more interested in whether the property really was your home and whether you really did live there rather than the length of time. So, the more evidence you have that it was your main residence, the more likely you are to convince him.

Evidence

- change your address with your local tax office. So, even his records will show that the property was your main residence!
- put utility and other bills in your own name at the property address. Typical bills include gas, electric, water, Council Tax and TV licence
- pay full Council Tax on the property
- register on the voters roll at the property
- change your address with your bank, so that all statements are delivered to the property address
- hire a removal van to move enough furniture from one house to the house you want to be your main residence. Keep receipts for any new furniture delivered to the property
- don't advertise the property for sale or rent until after the period of residence
- get building work done (e.g. have a new kitchen fitted) at your main home so you have to move out. Therefore, you can prove that you must be residing at the "investment" property.

5.5. CGT-AVOIDANCE STRATEGY: NOMINATE/FLIP A RESIDENCE

An unmarried individual or a married couple can only have one main residence for PPR relief at any one time. However, if you've got more than one home, it is possible to nominate which one you would like to be treated as your PPR. By doing this, it's possible to minimise the tax charge on both properties by switching your PPR between them. This practice is commonly known as "flipping" and has hit the headlines recently due to a number of MPs taking advantage of this legitimate tax avoidance strategy.

EXAMPLE

Colin owns a house in Bournemouth that he bought in 1985 for £100,000. In 2006, he also bought a house in Somerset for £250,000 which he uses mainly at the weekend. In 2013, Colin decides to sell the Somerset property for £350,000.

Without an election - the Taxman will treat his Bournemouth home as his PPR. There will be a gain of £100,000 before the annual exemption (2012/13 £10,600). As Colin is a higher rate taxpayer, this will give rise to a CGT bill of £25,032 (28% x (£100,000 – £10,600)).

With an election - when Colin bought the second property in 2006, he made an election to nominate his main residence. He elected the Bournemouth property. But in 2013, Colin made another election to switch the PPR exemption to the Somerset house. Under the "three year rule", the Somerset property is now exempt from CGT for the last three years of ownership. The gain is therefore reduced to 4/7ths £100,000, £57,143. After the annual exemption, his CGT bill is now £13,032. Therefore, by making a simple election he has saved himself tax of £12,000.

5.5.1.   How do I make the election?

The election must be made in writing to the Taxman and sent to your local tax office. See Appendix D for a sample election letter.

NOTE. In the case of a married couple, both partners must sign the election for it to be effective.

Time limit

From the date of purchasing or acquiring the second property, you have two years to tell the Taxman which one is your PPR.

TIP 1

You can extend the two-year limit by renting a flat for a few months as a third residence. Then you can elect one of the three properties within two years of starting to rent the flat.

TIP 2

Renting out one of the properties for a short period of time so it is no longer a PPR will also reset the election clock.

Changing the election

Once you've nominated a PPR, you can change or flip it by making a similar election in writing to the Taxman. The new election can be backdated by up to two years. See Appendix E for a sample variation of election letter.

TIP

When making the election, it's usually advantageous to choose the property that is most likely to make a bigger capital gain or be sold first. If you do end up selling the other one first, then you can simply change the election before you sell it.

Once the sale has been completed, the election is "flipped" back to the other home. That other home loses PPR relief but only for the period that it takes to actually sell the second property and is likely to be insignificant in a long period of ownership.

WARNING! In a falling market, it may not be beneficial to make a PPR election for a second home if a loss could be made when you sell it. Making a PPR election will reduce any capital loss available to be offset against other capital gains.

5.5.2. What happens if I don't make an election?

If you own two or more properties, and haven't told the Taxman which one is your main residence within the two-year time limit, he will make the decision for you based on, for example, the time spent in each property, or which is the main postal address.

It is possible that the Taxman might question whether the second property ever became a PPR so you will need evidence of occupation. As well as considering the factors in 5.4.1., it's worth keeping a diary showing the dates of overnight stays.

TIP

Make the election to nominate your PPR as soon as you acquire the second property. That way, you can make another election at any time in the future to switch your PPR.

WARNING! You will need to make a new election every time you have a new combination of two or more homes. For example, if you acquire a third home, you will need to make a new election.

5.5.3. How long does the nominated property have to be my PPR to qualify for relief?

As long as it qualifies as a residence, it doesn't matter how short you elect it as your PPR - as little as a week would be acceptable.

This is backed up by the Taxman's CGT manual which states that the election can be for "a short space of time" (http://www.hmrc.gov.uk/manuals/cgmanual/CG64510.htm).

5.6. SELLING LAND THAT IS PART OF YOUR MAIN RESIDENCE

A property developer may be interested in buying part of your home's garden in order to build new houses. So, if you decide to sell the land, do you have to pay CGT?

Half a hectare

If the total area of the grounds and garden (including the area on which the house itself stands) is less than half a hectare (just over an acre), then the Taxman will readily accept the land as being part of your main residence. Therefore, you will be able to claim full PPR relief and any gain will be exempt from CGT.

If the property was your home and has subsequently been let as private residential accommodation, then you can still claim partial PPR relief and private letting relief where the garden is less than half a hectare.

5.6.1. What happens if my garden is more than half a hectare?

If you've got more than half a hectare of grounds, you should argue an increase in the area that's classed as garden so that a larger area can be CGT-exempt. A number of taxpayers have tried to extend the half a hectare limit to reflect the size and character of their homes. The argument being that a larger area is required for the reasonable enjoyment of a larger house. Some have been successful, some not. If you manage to increase the exempt area, you also reduce the taxable area. If you think a bigger area is appropriate, then try and negotiate this with the Taxman (District Valuer) in advance.

> **TIP**
>
> The best evidence for this is if your neighbours have similar houses and similar sized gardens.

5.6.2. Would it be better to sell the property before I sell the land?

No. Case law has decided that if you sell your main residence before you sell the land, then you are unable to claim PPR relief on the sale of the land. This is because the land is no longer attached to your main residence. So, if you were thinking of moving or now don't fancy living next to a building site, be very careful what you sell first.

Tɪᴘ

So you don't lose your PPR exemption:

- sell the land wanted for building before you sell the house and remaining garden
- do not let development work take place before the land is sold
- do not fence off the development plot until it is sold.

5.6.3. CGT-avoidance strategy: develop and move

Problem

Rather than just sell off part of your garden, you want to maximise profits by developing it first (i.e. building a new house in the grounds) and then selling it off. However, this will mean that the developed land is no longer part of your main residence and therefore much of your profit could be swallowed up by a hefty tax bill.

Solution

Move into the newly built property and sell your old house. Your old property will qualify for full PPR relief as long as it's sold within three years (the "three year rule" 5.1.4.). You will also be entitled to full PPR relief on your new house as long as you move in within twelve months of the development starting (5.1.6.).

5.7. MAKING USE OF YOUR CHILDREN

Every unmarried individual can have a main residence and this includes your children. And, if they have a main residence, they will be entitled to claim PPR relief when they sell the property.

If you have children going away to college or university or starting a job in another part of the country, then you may want to buy them a house nearby as both an investment for their future and somewhere semi-decent for them to live. If you decide to do this, make sure that it is structured correctly to make maximum use of various reliefs.

The property should be purchased in your child's name and they should have beneficial and legal title. There shouldn't be a problem getting finance for this as long as you are prepared to put down the deposit and act as guarantor on the mortgage. The rental income received from letting spare rooms to, for example, other students should be sufficient to cover the mortgage repayments. Your child will also be able to claim "rent-a-room" relief on the rental income so there will be no tax for them to pay on the first £4,250 of rental profits (see 1.4.).

As long as the property is your child's only property, it will be regarded as their main residence and PPR relief will be available on the sale of it.

NOTE. The Taxman will generally accept that taking in lodgers does not restrict the availability of PPR. A "lodger" is someone who, whilst having their own bedroom, will otherwise live as part of the owner's household. Student friends would, therefore, qualify as lodgers.

5.7.1. Can I receive any of the proceeds once my child has sold the property?

This technique should only be used if you are happy to pass on wealth to your children. However, as long as you give the mortgage deposit to your child with no strings attached and they are not contractually obligated to give you a share of the proceeds, then technically there is no reason why they can't make a generous gift to you once they have sold the property! But be aware that this may be challenged by the Taxman.

6. The tax implications of gifting properties

6.1. AVOIDING CGT WHEN TRANSFERRING PROPERTY TO SOMEONE OTHER THAN YOUR SPOUSE

Spouses can freely transfer ownership of properties between each other without having to pay Capital Gains Tax (CGT). Unfortunately, the same exemption does not apply to unmarried or unregistered couples. However, with some careful planning, you can still transfer properties to an unmarried partner, your children, or anyone else for that matter, tax-free.

6.1.1. Make use of the annual exemption and transfer in stages

If you want to transfer a residential investment property (i.e. it's not your principal private residence) to someone other than a spouse, then consider doing it in stages over a number of years. You can then take advantage of your annual CGT allowance to wipe out your CGT bill.

EXAMPLE

Sue and Paul bought an investment property for £55,000 in June 2008 with the intention of giving it to their two daughters Valerie and Lucy in 2012/13 when they are both over 18. However, in 2012/13, the property is worth £150,000. So, if they transfer the property to their daughters now, as higher rate taxpayers they are facing a £20,664 CGT bill ((£150,000 - £55,000) - (2 x £10,600) x 28%).

Therefore, they decide to transfer £10,600 (7.1%) of the property to each of their daughters in 2012/13 in order to make use of each of their annual CGT allowances but without triggering a CGT bill. In 2013/14, they will make another transfer of the property to their daughters equal to that year's annual allowance. They will continue doing this until they have transferred the entire property tax-free.

NOTE. The part transfer of property can be tricky so make sure you get yourself a good solicitor and weigh up the legal costs versus the savings.

6.1.2. What about Stamp Duty?

There is no Stamp Duty Land Tax (SDLT) on gifts of property providing the outstanding mortgage being transferred is not more than £125,000. However, if the mortgage on the property is over £125,000, there will be SDLT to pay, even for CGT-exempt transfers between spouses.

EXAMPLE

Thomas owns a buy-to-let property worth £500,000, on which there is a mortgage of £400,000. He gives half of the property to his wife. There will be no CGT to pay because gifts between spouses are free of CGT, but his wife will have to pay SDLT. Having taken over half the mortgage (£200,000), she is deemed to have "paid" that for her half share in the house, and SDLT of £2,000 is due (1% x £200,000).

6.2. HOW TO AVOID CGT ON GIFTS OF HOLIDAY HOMES

The normal rules for residential investment properties are that if you give your property away to anyone other than your spouse, then you have to pay CGT based on the market value of the property at the date of the gift. However, if you've got a property that qualifies as a furnished holiday home (see 3.2. for qualifying criteria), then you may be able to take advantage of the very generous "gift (also known as "holdover") relief". By claiming this relief, you can avoid paying CGT when you give a property to, for example, an unmarried partner or your children.

6.2.1. What is "gift relief"?

When you dispose of a qualifying holiday home, you can ask for the capital gain to be "held over". In other words, the capital gain is passed on to the person you give the property to. This is achieved by them being treated as purchasing the property at its original cost to you. Therefore, when they eventually sell the property, they will pay tax on any increase in value from the date you purchased the property and not from the date you gave it to them.

6.2.2. How do I make a claim?

You can make a claim by using the form on the back of the Taxman's help sheet HS295 available from http://www.hmrc.gov.uk/helpsheets/hs295.pdf. This form needs to be signed by both you and the person you give the property to.

You don't have to include a calculation of the gain with your claim as long as you complete the second page of the form.

6.2.3. Is there a time limit for making the claim?

You need to make a claim within four years of the end of the tax year in which you make the gift. So, if you make a gift in July 2012, you have until April 5 2017 to make the claim.

6.2.4. So how will it work if I want to give a holiday home to one of my children?

You have a furnished holiday home that you would like to give to one of your children without paying CGT. When you give them the property, you both need to sign a "gift relief election" (see 6.2.2.). This will mean that your child is deemed to have acquired the property at a price equal to what you paid for it. You are deemed to have sold the holiday home at that price. So, there's no CGT for you to pay because your sale price equals your purchase price.

6.2.5. But doesn't this mean that my child will pay more CGT when they eventually sell the property?

Not necessarily. If your child lives in the property and makes it (or nominates it as) their main residence (see 5.4.1. for guidance on how to do this), there could be no CGT to pay when they sell the property.

There will be no CGT to pay as long as the property was your child's main residence throughout their period of ownership. In this case, the total gain that they would have paid tax on is exempt. And, due to the gift relief election, this total gain will include any gain arising during your period of ownership.

6.2.6. Can I receive any of the proceeds once my child has sold the property?

This would be the ultimate tax avoidance; selling the property via your child and converting a large taxable gain into a tax-free one. Therefore, it's likely to be looked at very closely by the Taxman. However, as long as you make the gift to your child absolute i.e. with no strings attached, it would be difficult for him to make a successful challenge. Of course, this doesn't prevent your child from making a generous gift to you some time in the future!

6.2.7. CGT-avoidance strategy - don't gift the holiday home, sell it at undervalue

The problem with giving a property away is that you won't receive any proceeds (unless your offspring are generous enough to give you part of the proceeds later!). So, rather than give the property away, you could sell it at undervalue. However, where you sell at undervalue, the gain that is held over is reduced by the excess of the sale proceeds over the cost. By selling at the right price and signing a gift relief exemption, you could still avoid CGT altogether.

NOTE. When a property is transferred or sold to a "connected person", the estimated market value at the time of sale/transfer must be used when calculating the CGT liability, instead of the amount paid. Hence the reason that there is still a gain to holdover when selling at undervalue.

Connected persons are:

*   business partners
*   mother, father, or more remote ancestor
*   daughter, son or more remote descendant
*   brothers and sisters
*   those who are regarded as close family by marriage, i.e. in-laws.

The right price

Sell the property for a price equal to the total of:

*   your original purchase price
*   the costs of improvements
*   the annual exemption.

By doing this, you'll have no tax to pay as you can elect to holdover the whole gain. The proceeds do not exceed the cost.

EXAMPLE

Mary and Anthony jointly own a holiday cottage in the Cotswolds which qualifies as a furnished holiday home. They have now decided to sell the home to their daughter, Olivia, at a price that will mean they pay no CGT. They originally purchased the cottage in 2000 for £80,000 and it is now worth £300,000. They can make a claim to holdover the gain and avoid CGT if they sell the property for a price less than or equal to the cost of £80,000 plus their annual exemptions (2 x £10,600). The gain that's held over will be £198,800 and the allowable cost to Olivia will be £101,200, i.e. what she paid. As higher rate taxpayers, by holding over the gain Mary and Anthony will save £55,644 (£198,800 x 28%) in tax. If Olivia then lives in the property as her main residence, she can sell the cottage tax-free.

Be careful. Mary and Anthony will need to avoid any personal use of the cottage after their gift to Olivia or they could be liable to a pre-owned assets income tax charge.

6.2.8. Do furnished holiday homes qualify for entrepreneurs' relief?

A business of commercial letting of furnished holiday accommodation in the UK is treated as a trade. This means that the sale of a furnished holiday home should qualify for entrepreneurs' relief.

This relief works by simply applying a reduced rate of CGT of 10% on the first £10 million of lifetime gains on disposal of furnished holiday homes and certain other trade assets such as shares in a personal company. However, it does not apply to the sale of commercial investment properties.

To make sure the furnished holiday home qualifies for the relief, you need to ensure that:

- the property is still being used as a qualifying furnished holiday home at the time of sale; or

- the property is sold within three years of ceasing to be used as a qualifying furnished holiday home.

More than one furnished holiday home?

The Taxman takes the view that unless the assets sold can themselves be operated as a business, they won't qualify for entrepreneurs' relief. In our view, a furnished holiday home is capable of being run separately from any other furnished holiday homes you may have and, therefore, it would be very difficult for the Taxman to argue that it didn't qualify for the reduced 10% CGT rate.

6.3. USING TRUSTS TO AVOID CGT

Usually, as a property investor, you can only claim gift relief (6.2.1.) when you transfer furnished holiday accommodation to someone else. It's not generally available to landlords renting residential or commercial properties (although there are exceptions where it is used in your trade). However, you can avoid paying CGT on any type of property by transferring it into certain types of trust.

6.3.1. What is a trust?

A trust is formed when one person (the settlor) gives some assets to somebody else (the trustee) to use for the benefit of others (the beneficiaries). There are two main types of trust, discretionary (also known as "mainstream" trusts) and non-discretionary. For property purposes, the most common non-discretionary trust is a "qualifying interest in possession" trust.

Up to March 21 2006, gift relief was only available for transfers into discretionary trusts. From March 22 2006, gift relief is also available for transfers into most interest in possession trusts created on or after that date.

6.3.2. What's the difference between a discretionary trust and an interest in possession trust?

As its name suggests, in a discretionary trust, the trustees have discretion in deciding when and to whom (of the beneficiaries) payments of trust income or capital are made. No beneficiary has the right to demand income from a discretionary trust.

With an interest in possession trust, the beneficiary has an immediate and automatic right to the income from the trust after expenses. The trustee must pass all of the net income received to the beneficiary. The beneficiary who receives income (the "income beneficiary") often doesn't have any rights over the capital held in such a trust. The capital will normally pass to a different beneficiary or beneficiaries in the future.

Therefore, a discretionary trust gives more flexibility for tax planning purposes.

6.3.3. Does a discretionary trust have to pay tax on its income and gains?

Yes. The discretionary trust is subject to income tax and CGT in the same way as individuals. However, above the first £1,000 of income, the downside is that this type of trust is taxed at the highest rate of tax:

- first £1,000 of income is taxed at the basic rate of 20% (10%) for dividends
- income above £1,000 is taxed at the "additional rate" (i.e. 50% for 2012/13 (42.5% for dividends)
- capital gains are taxed at the higher rate of 28%.

Trusts have an annual CGT exemption which is half that of an individual (i.e. £5,300 for 2012/13).

TIP

Although discretionary trusts pay income tax at the highest rate of tax, when the trustees make a payment to a beneficiary, that payment is grossed up at the trust tax rate so that the beneficiary gets a tax credit at that rate. So if the trustees make a payment to a beneficiary who is a non or basic rate taxpayer, they can claim a tax refund.

The trustees have to complete a tax return in exactly the same way as individuals. The filing deadlines and tax payment dates are also the same.

A discretionary trust may also have to pay Inheritance Tax (IHT) if its value is more than the IHT nil-rate band (£325,000 for 2012/13). On every tenth anniversary there will be a charge of no more than 6% of the trust value and, at eventual exit, a further maximum 6% charge.

6.3.4. How do I set up a discretionary trust?

Anyone over 18 can set up a trust in the UK to hold UK property. A solicitor should be able to set one up (by drafting a trust deed) for you for around £250 to £500 plus VAT.

6.3.5. How do I put the property into a discretionary trust?

You can transfer the property into a trust as a gift. As with gifts to other people, the property is treated as being transferred at its market value.

However, you can elect to have this gain held-over (see 6.2.1.), which means that you won't pay any CGT.

NOTE. Any transfer into a discretionary trust is a chargeable transfer for IHT purposes (see 6.5.). This means that if you transfer a property into a discretionary trust, you may have to pay IHT of 20%. However, provided the value of the property is less than the nil-rate band (£325,000 for 2012/13), you will avoid paying tax on the transfer.

6.4.   TAX-AVOIDANCE STRATEGY - USING TRUSTS TO DEFER CGT ON RESIDENTIAL PROPERTY GIFTS

Problem

If you have an investment property that you have never lived in, it's likely that you will pay CGT on any gain you make when you transfer it.

Solution

As long as the property is worth less than £325,000, you can transfer it into a discretionary trust without paying any CGT or IHT. As the settlor, you would elect for any gain from the gift into the trust to be held-over.

Therefore, you have deferred the CGT liability, but the gain will still be chargeable on any subsequent disposal by the beneficiary (or beneficiaries).

NOTE. If you gift a property to a trust in which you have some sort of interest, then, since December 10 2003, you cannot claim gift relief.

Avoiding tax on property disposals

6.4.1. Can the trust beneficiaries live in the property and claim PPR relief?

No. Before December 10 2003, there was a specific tax avoidance scheme where a discretionary trust was used to defer a gain on a property that is then occupied by one of the beneficiaries as their main residence. On disposal of the property by the trustees the whole gain is exempt from CGT under the main residence exemption rules. However, since December 2003, either the gain on transfer to the trust can be deferred or PPR relief can subsequently be claimed, but not both.

TIP

Consider not electing to hold over the gain on the original transfer into the trust but opting to pay CGT sooner rather than later, especially if it is thought that CGT rates are likely to rise in future.

6.5. INHERITANCE TAX ON LIFETIME GIFTS

As you are probably aware, you may have to pay Inheritance Tax (IHT) on the value of your estate (basically everything you own - all your assets minus anything you owe) when you die. You also have to pay IHT on certain gifts you make while you are alive. These are known as "chargeable lifetime transfers" and occur when you gift an asset into a discretionary trust (see 6.3.2.).

Also, if you decide to gift a property to someone else without putting it into a discretionary trust, then the person you are gifting the property to could incur IHT on the gift if you die within seven years of making the gift. These are known as "potentially exempt transfers" (PETs).

Therefore, before you decide to gift properties, it is important to understand the potential IHT implications.

6.5.1. What are the basic principles of IHT?

IHT is a tax charged on the value of your property and other assets in your estate at the date of death, less any outstanding loans. IHT on death is charged at the following rates:

- on the first £325,000 (2012/13) - 0%

- on the balance of the estate over £325,000 (2012/13) - 40% (or 36% if 10% or more of the estate is left to charity).

The first £325,000 of your estate is known as the "nil-rate band".

IHT on "chargeable lifetime transfers", i.e. gifts into discretionary and some other trusts, is charged at 20% if over the "nil-rate band".

Exempt gifts

Certain gifts are exempt from IHT altogether. These include:

- gifts between UK domiciled spouses and civil partners (if your spouse is not domiciled in the UK, then the exemption is restricted to £55,000)
- gifts to UK registered charities.

Seven-year rule

Any gifts you make, apart from transfers into chargeable trusts, are IHT-free as long as you manage to survive seven years after making the gift (a PET). If you die within seven years, the recipients will have to pay IHT, but on a sliding scale. If you die within three years, they have to pay 40% of anything above the nil-rate band. If, however, you die after three years, the tax reduces by 20% for each additional year survived.

6.5.2. Can I give a property away, but continue to live in it?

No, the property must be given outright. For instance, if you give your house to your children, but carry on living in it without paying the full market rent, that would be a gift with "reservation of benefit". This would still be counted as part of your estate when you die even if you live more than seven years.

Market rent

If you do want to continue living in a property, then you need to make sure that you pay a market rent for the privilege. A local firm of surveyors would be able to provide a suitable rent value.

NOTE. The rent will be taxable income on the new owners of the home.

TIP

Rather than give away the whole house, you could give away a proportion of it to one of your children who then lives there with you and shares the running costs. Providing your child doesn't move out, your estate will be reduced by the amount given away providing you live more than seven years.

6.5.3. How does IHT interact with CGT?

As long as you give away your properties more than seven years before you die then you will avoid IHT. However, gifting property during your lifetime will result in a CGT charge on any gains. You can avoid CGT by not gifting properties during your lifetime, but then your estate will suffer IHT on any amounts over £325,000 (2012/13). So, you always need to consider both IHT and CGT in deciding whether to transfer properties to someone other than your spouse.

6.6. IHT (AND CGT) AVOIDANCE STRATEGY: EQUITY RELEASE

In 4.3, we looked at a CGT-avoidance strategy where you can withdraw funds from your investment properties by re-mortgaging the properties rather than selling them. This can also be a very effective way of limiting the amount of IHT you have to pay.

Problem

You've built up a decent portfolio of investment properties and you now want to pass this on to your children. However, if you just gift them the properties, you will have to pay CGT on any gains you've made. So, how can you transfer the properties to your children, avoiding CGT and IHT in the process?

Solution

For IHT purposes, the value of your properties included in your estate is their market value less any outstanding loans. So, you mortgage up to the hilt on your properties, and then gift the cash raised to the children. Cash is not a capital asset, so there's no CGT to pay on the transfer.

Provided you survive seven years from the date of the transfer, there will also be no IHT to pay on it. Therefore, you have reduced the value of your estate and IHT will only be payable on the net value of the properties (you've re-mortgaged so the high level of borrowings will keep the IHT bill down) The downside is that you will have to pay mortgage interest.

When should I re-mortgage?

Deciding when to re-mortgage your properties and give away the cash is a difficult balancing act. Ideally, you have to pitch it so that you're young enough to have the maximum chance of surviving seven years, but not so young that it is difficult to decide how much you can afford to give away without depriving yourself of a decent lifestyle.

While your children may very well be willing to hand back any money you need later on, they may not be able to do so. They may, for instance, have lost it in a divorce settlement or simply frittered it away.

Alternative solution

If you are concerned about giving cash to your children or surviving seven years, then you could re-mortgage and invest the money in assets that do not attract IHT such as shares in unlisted trading companies or let agricultural land. After two years, these types of assets qualify for 100% IHT relief.

6.7.   TAX-AVOIDANCE STRATEGY: TRANSFERS TO SPOUSE

The IHT rules were changed quite significantly for spouses and civil partners where the surviving spouse died on or after October 9 2007. From this date, where one party (e.g. the husband) dies and leaves all his estate to his wife, there would be no IHT on the husband's death because gifts to spouses are exempt (see 6.5.1.). In the past, the husband would have wasted his nil-rate band as shown in the following example:

EXAMPLE

Ozzie and Harriet make wills leaving their respective estates to each other and then to their children on the death of the survivor. Ozzie has assets worth £300,000 and Harriet also has assets worth £300,000. Ozzie dies before Harriet.

On Ozzie's death, his £300,000 estate passes to Harriet and there is no IHT to pay as transfers to spouses are exempt from IHT.

On Harriet's death, her estate is now worth £600,000 (her estate of £300,000 plus £300,000 inherited from Ozzie). Therefore, the IHT payable will be £110,000 (40% (£600,000 the 2012/13 nil-rate band of £325,000).

However, it is now possible for the estate of the second spouse (e.g. the widow), on her death, to claim not only her nil-rate band but also any unused nil-rate band of her husband.

EXAMPLE

Let's say Ozzie died on January 3 2008 and left the whole of his estate to his wife, Harriet. If she dies in October 2012, the available nil-rate band is now her own £325,000 plus that not used on her husband's death, up rated to the 2012/13 level, i.e. £325,000 so that the total nil-rate band becomes £650,000.

A claim has to be made to transfer the nil-rate band using Form IHT 216 (http:// www.hmrc.gov.uk/CTO/iht216.pdf). The claim has to be made within 24 months from the end the month of the death of the second spouse.

Problem

Before this tax advantage for spouses came in, it had always been advisable to ensure that on the death of the first spouse, an amount equal to the nil-rate band was transferred either directly to, for example, the children or grandchildren or into a discretionary trust. With the new rule this is less likely to be necessary and may in fact be a disadvantage.

EXAMPLE

Taking the example above, Ozzie's will left the nil-rate band amount to his children and any remainder to his wife. Therefore, on his death, £300,000 (the 2007/8 nil-rate band) was left to his children. When Harriet died in October 2012, her estate was worth £340,000. As Ozzie has used up all his nil-rate band in his will, the IHT payable on Harriet's death will be £6,000 ((£340,000 less £325,000) x 40%). However, if Ozzie had left all his estate to his wife, there would have been no IHT to pay on Harriet's death as she would have had a total estate of £640,000 which would have been covered by the joint nil-rate band available (£325,000 x 2).

Action

If you made your will before October 9 2007, then it is important to review it as soon as possible particularly as it could now be sensible to minimise transfers to, for example, your children on the first death, given that the nil-rate band will continue to enjoy increases each year. By doing this, you can maximise the nil-rate band on the second death. Soon after the first death, the surviving spouse can then make gifts to, for example, their children or a trust, in the hope of reducing the value of their estate before their death.

SECTION III

Buying strategies to avoid tax

7. Buying a property in joint names

Many people buy their first investment property in their sole name. However, buying a property jointly can have significant tax savings. This chapter looks at the tax effects of owning a property jointly, firstly with your with your spouse, and then with someone else.

7.1. JOINT OWNERSHIP WITH YOUR SPOUSE

Owning property in joint names with your spouse can lead to both income tax and Capital Gains Tax (CGT) savings. This is particularly true where one of you is a higher rate taxpayer and the other has little, or no, income.

7.1.1. Can I save income tax on my rental profits if I transfer the property to my spouse?

Sole owner

If you are the sole owner of a property and let it out, you have to pay tax on any profit (rent less expenses) you make (see 1.2.). The rate of income tax depends on your total income during the tax year. For 2012/13, if your other income is more than £42,475 then you will be paying tax at the higher rate of 40% unless your income is over £150,000 when you will pay tax at the "additional rate" of 50%.

> EXAMPLE 1
>
> Peter is a director of a company and receives a salary of £60,000. He also has an investment property which he rents out for £500 a month (£6,000 a year). His rental expenses for the year were £2,000. Therefore, Peter has to pay tax of £1,600 on his rental income ((£6,000 - £2,000) x 40%).

Transfer to spouse

If one of you is a higher rate taxpayer whilst the other is not paying any tax at all (or paying tax at the basic rate), then you can make significant income tax savings by transferring the investment property either into joint names or into the sole name of the spouse with the lower income. Your spouse will not be taxed at the higher rate on their rental income until their total income for the year exceeds £42,475 (2012/13).

EXAMPLE 2

Peter's wife, Sam, doesn't work and has no other income. Peter decides to transfer the property into her name. As Sam has no other income, the whole £4,000 rental profit is covered by her tax-free personal allowance (£8,105 for 2012/13). As there is no tax to pay on the rental profits, they save £1,600.

If Sam has a job and earns £20,000 a year, it would still be beneficial for Peter to transfer the property into her name. In this case, she would pay 20% tax on the rental profits of £4,000, still a saving of £800 (£1,600 - £800).

Joint ownership

There may be situations where it is preferable for you to each have a share in the property. For example, you may both be basic rate taxpayers with similar income. However, if you were the sole owner of the property, the rental income would take you into the higher rate band. By owning the property jointly, you both have a share of the rental income and stay below the higher rate band.

EXAMPLE 3

Peter has a salary of £42,000 a year and Sam's is £25,000. The rental income from the investment property is £4,000 a year. If Peter were the sole owner of the property, he would pay 20% tax on the first £475 of rental income (taking his total income for the year up to the £42,475 threshold), but would pay 40% tax on the remainder. Therefore, the tax on his rental income would be £1,505.

If Peter and Sam jointly own the property, then the rental income will be split between them. In this case, all of Sam's share will be taxed at 20% and the first £475 of Peter's will be. Assuming the rental income is split equally, owning the property jointly has saved them £400 (£2,000 x 20%) a year.

NOTE. If you are both higher rate taxpayers, there are no income tax advantages to buying the property with your spouse. However, there could still be significant CGT savings (see 7.1.4.).

7.1.2.   If I own a property jointly with my spouse, do we always have to split the rental profits equally?

There are situations where it may be preferable to split the income in unequal proportions.

EXAMPLE

Taking Example 3 above, it would be preferable for Sam to have a greater share of the rental profits so that she can avoid paying any higher rate tax. If Peter received 10% (£400) of the profits with Sam receiving 90% (£3,600), then neither of them would pay tax at the higher rate and their total tax bill would be £800. A saving of £305 compared with sharing the profits equally.

The problem is that where you hold a property jointly with your spouse, the Taxman automatically treats you and your spouse as sharing the income 50:50. This is the case even if you don't actually own the investment in equal shares.

However, if you don't own the property in equal proportions, you can jointly elect to be taxed on your actual shares. To do this you must both complete and sign a "declaration" form (Form 17 which you can download from http://www.hmrc.gov.uk/forms/form17.pdf) and send it to the Taxman. The declaration takes effect from the date it is made, providing you send it to the Taxman within 60 days.

Evidence

Unfortunately, it's not enough just to make the declaration, you have to give the Taxman proof of anything other than a 50:50 split. This means that if you want a 75:25 split of the rental profits, you need to show that the property is owned 75:25.

However, it seems that different tax offices are asking for different information. Some will accept a signed declaration by both parties that ownership of the joint asset is no longer 50:50 but now some other proportion. Other tax offices want copies of more formal property documents, such as "declaration of trust" (see 7.2.5.). Our advice is to send in just a signed declaration, but be ready to provide further information if requested.

7.1.3.   Tax-avoidance strategy: Split the income but retain ownership

Problem

As mentioned in 7.1.1., transferring the property either partly or wholly to your lower income spouse can lead to considerable income tax savings. However, this tax planning is only effective when the beneficial title in the property is genuinely transferred to your spouse. The problem is that you may not want to give your spouse a large share in the property. So, how can you save income tax on your rental profits without giving up too much of your ownership of the property?

Solution

If you solely own a property, follow these steps to retain majority ownership, and pay less income tax - the best of both worlds!

1. Transfer the property into joint ownership (see 7.2. and seek advice from your solicitor).

2. Transfer only 1% beneficial ownership to your spouse, so that you retain 99% ownership.

3. Don't elect for the income to be split by the beneficial ownership percentages.

Under the 50:50 rule, tax law automatically treats you as sharing the income equally even if you don't actually own the investment in equal shares.

7.1.4. Can I save CGT if I own the property jointly with my spouse?

By owning a property with your spouse, you can also make substantial tax savings when you come to sell the property. This is because each individual has an annual CGT allowance, currently £10,600 for 2012/13 (see 4.1.5.). Therefore, you and your spouse can each use the exemption to reduce your part of the gain. So, when you sell the property, the first £21,200 of the gain (assuming no other gains in the year) will be tax-free.

EXAMPLE

Adam solely owns an investment property which has made a capital gain of £50,000 when he comes to sell it in September 2012. As Adam is a higher rate taxpayer, he will pay tax on the gain of £11,032 (28% x (£50,000 - £10,600)).

However, if Adam and his wife, Natalie jointly own the property, then they each have an annual exemption to offset against the gain. Therefore, the maximum tax on the gain will be £8,064 (28% x (£50,000 - £21,200)). A saving of £2,968 (£10,600 x 28%).

7.1.5. If I own a property jointly with my spouse, will the capital gains automatically be split 50:50?

No. The capital gain will be split according to the proportion of ownership. So, if you own 75% of the property, you will be allocated 75% of the gain.

7.1.6. Can I transfer half the property to my spouse before I sell it to make use of their annual exemption?

Yes, you can. Spouses can transfer ownership of properties between each other without incurring CGT (see 4.1.4.). Just make sure that you have a non-tax avoidance reason for doing so (e.g. it was a birthday present) and that the transfer is made before putting the property on the market.

WARNING! You are likely to incur costs when you transfer a property. Solicitors' fees are usually around £300 to do the transfer and your mortgage lender may charge a fee to issue the mortgage in joint names. But the most significant cost is likely to be Stamp Duty as transfers between spouses are not exempt from this. However, Stamp Duty will only be payable if the property is mortgaged and you are transferring more than £125,000 of the mortgage amount to your partner.

7.2. HOW DO I TRANSFER PART OF A PROPERTY TO MY SPOUSE?

If you decide to transfer a property to your spouse (or anyone else for that matter), then you will need to let your solicitor know what type of joint ownership you want.

7.2.1. What are the different types of joint ownership?

NOTE. The legal terms used to describe the different types of ownership make reference to "tenants". This makes it seem as though it's about rented property. This is not the case - it's just legal jargon!

If you decide to own a house jointly with someone else (whether it's your spouse, partner, relative or friend), you can own it in one of two ways - as joint tenants or tenants-in-common.

Joint tenants

Here, the joint owners do not have particular shares in the property; they own the whole thing together. When one owner dies, the property automatically becomes the possession of the other owner(s). Because no joint owner has a defined share, their interest in the property does not become part of their estate when they die, but simply disappears. This means that a will made by the first joint tenant to die, which leaves the property to someone else, would be ineffective.

A husband and wife are normally treated as owning joint property as joint tenants so they have equal rights over the property and when one dies, the other automatically owns all of it.

If you own a property as joint tenants then your rental profits and capital gains will be divided equally between you.

Tenants-in-common

Each owner has a defined share of the property. They can decide between themselves what proportion of the property belongs to each owner. When the property is sold, each owner is entitled to his or her percentage share of the sale proceeds. If one of the owners dies, their share is added to their estate and does not automatically pass to the other tenants-in-common.

NOTE. If you don't specify that you want different shares then the law assumes that the shares are equal i.e. if there are two owners, this will automatically be half each, if three owners, a third each and so on.

It's only if you and your spouse own a property in unequal shares as tenants-in-common, that you can elect to have your rental profits split in the proportions of your ownership (see 7.1.2.). Any capital gain will automatically be divided between you according to your proportion of ownership (see 7.1.5.).

7.2.2. Which method should I use?

Joint tenants

This is most suitable for you and your spouse where the combined value of your properties is likely to be under two times the Inheritance Tax threshold (i.e. under £650,000 for 2012/13). If you have a main residence and separate buy-to-let investment properties, this may not be the case.

Tenants-in-common

This is more suitable form of ownership when:

- you are not married to the other owners (e.g. family, friends, business associates, unmarried partners) or
- the combined value of you and your spouse's property is over twice the Inheritance Tax threshold (i.e. over £650,000 for 2012/13) or
- you need to have unequal shares in a property, for example to save income tax (7.1.2.).

NOTE. You may be able to change from joint tenants to tenants-in-common at a later date, but you will not be able to change back from tenants-in-common to joint tenants.

7.2.3. How do I change from joint tenants to tenants-in-common?

If you currently own the property as joint tenants then it is relatively simple to change to tenants-in-common. However, we would recommend that you seek advice from a solicitor before doing this.

WARNING! Consider the consequences of severing a joint tenancy carefully. If you are actually living in the property and choose to sever the joint tenancy, the death of your partner could mean that you are prematurely forced to sell the house. You will not automatically receive your partner's share in the property should he or she die, as would have been the case had the joint tenancy been preserved.

This can, of course, be overcome by making sure that your partner's share of the property is left to you in their will, but you may not want to do this for Inheritance Tax reasons. In the past few years it has been a popular way to ensure that the nil-rate band of the first spouse to die is utilised as they passed their share to, say, their children. However, since the changes to the IHT rules for spouses it may no longer be advisable to do so. Always seek professional advice before doing this.

Notice of severance

To change from joint tenants to tenants-in-common, all you need to do is to give the other person a formal notice of severance (they don't have to agree). This must be in writing, and all that is necessary to say is:

> "I *(insert name)* give notice to *(insert names of other co-owners)* of my intention to sever the joint tenancy of *(insert address)*. Dated *(insert date)*"

and make sure you sign it!

Send it by recorded or registered post.

Changing shares

Unless the severance notice says otherwise, the joint tenancy will become a tenancy-in-common in equal shares. You can change the actual proportion of ownership by asking your solicitor to draw up a separate declaration of trust.

7.2.4. What should be included in a declaration of trust (trust deed)?

If the way in which you choose to own your property is as tenants-in-common then you should have a declaration of trust. This records the arrangement between the joint owners.

The trust deed should state:

- the percentage share that each owner has, i.e. you might say that one person has a 25% share and the other has a 75% share and that if the property were sold then the money would be divided in that way

- if there is a mortgage on the property, then the trust deed should provide for this to be paid off before dividing the sale proceeds. The trust deed should also define the proportions in which the two owners would make the mortgage payments.

7.2.5. Should I transfer part of the mortgage debt to my spouse?

If you transfer part of the property to your spouse and they also take over responsibility for part of the mortgage, then that proportion is treated as sale proceeds and Stamp Duty Land Tax (see 10.2.) will be due on the transfer unless the mortgage transferred is less than £125,000.

TIP

When you transfer a proportion of the property to your spouse, make sure you don't transfer the mortgage. This way you will avoid Stamp Duty Land Tax on the transfer.

7.3. JOINT OWNERSHIP WITH SOMEONE OTHER THAN YOUR SPOUSE

7.3.1. Can I save income tax if I transfer the property to someone other than my spouse?

Yes, you can. However, the problem is that you can't usually transfer a property to a non-spouse without incurring a potential CGT bill (see 4.1.3.). Therefore, it would be better to buy a property in joint names from the outset, rather than transfer it at a later date.

Once the property is in joint names, the income tax savings are the same as for joint ownership between spouses (see 7.1.1.). Again, you will make the largest income tax savings where you are a higher rate taxpayer and your co-owner (or owners) pays no tax or tax at the basic rate.

7.3.2. How is the income split if I own a property with someone other than my spouse?

As mentioned in 7.1.2, all property jointly owned between spouses is treated as an equal 50:50 split unless they make an election otherwise. However, this is not the case for property owned between non-spouses. In this situation, the split of income is based on the proportion of ownership in the property.

7.3.3. Can I save CGT if I own a property with someone other than my spouse?

Yes. The CGT savings on sale of a property are exactly the same as for spouses (see 7.1.4.). Again, any gain will be split according to the proportion of ownership.

7.3.4. Can I transfer half the property to someone before I sell it to make use of their annual exemption?

As mentioned in 7.3.1., where you transfer a property to someone other than your spouse, the market value of the property at the time of the transfer must be used to work out any taxable capital gain. However, by transferring a property into joint names with someone other than your spouse prior to sale could still save you CGT.

EXAMPLE

Jack bought an investment property several years ago and has now decided to sell. He estimates that the capital gain will be £120,000, so he would be facing a CGT bill of £30,632 (assuming the 2012/13 CGT allowance of £10,600) when he sells the property.

Therefore, Jack decides to transfer half the property to his son, Matthew, in the 2012/13 tax year. When he makes the transfer, he will have to pay CGT on the market value of the amount transferred (i.e. half of the total value of the property). He will, therefore, have a CGT bill of £13,832 ((£60,000 - £10,600) x 28%) when he makes the transfer.

In 2012/13, both Jack and Matthew decide to jointly sell the property. The property hasn't increased much in value since last year so Matthew will pay no CGT on his share of the gain. Assuming the annual exemption stayed the same, Jack would have another CGT bill for £13,832. Therefore, Jack has made an overall tax saving of £2,968 (28% of the annual exemption of £10,600).

NOTE. Transferring a property to someone else has possible Inheritance Tax implications (see 6.5.). And as in 7.1.6. make sure you have a non-tax avoidance reason for making the transfer or the Taxman might try to challenge the arrangement.

7.3.5. Can I own a property jointly with more than one person?

Yes, you can. In this case, the potential tax savings could be even greater as any gain on the eventual sale would be divided between the different partners with each partner being able to use their annual CGT allowance. If you're all higher rate taxpayers, selling a property jointly owned by you and three other people could save you up to £8,904 in CGT in 2012/13 ((£10,600 x 3) x 28%).

You can only register a maximum of four legal owners of a property with the Land Registry (or show four legal owners on the title deeds if the property isn't registered). However, you could have more than four tenants-in-common (i.e. more than four beneficial owners), each entitled to a proportion of the proceeds when the property is sold (as detailed in a declaration of trust - see 7.2.4.).

7.3.6. Does a mortgage on the property have to be in the names of all the owners?

A lender will require the mortgage to be a charge over the legal title of the property. If the legal title is in joint names, then the mortgage will also have to be in joint names.

However, as it is possible for someone to be a beneficial owner without being a legal owner, the mortgage doesn't have to be in the name of all the owners.

8. Owning properties through a limited company

III

One of the most commonly asked tax questions is whether holding properties in a limited company, rather than as an individual or partnership, will save tax. Unfortunately, there isn't a definitive answer as it depends on a large number of factors, such as your personal circumstances and how long you intend to hold the properties. Any future changes in legislation could also affect the decision.

8.1. WHAT IS A LIMITED COMPANY?

A company has a separate legal status to its owners. This means that if you use a company to buy a property, its name will appear on the title deeds rather than yours. The ownership of a company depends on who holds its shares (the shareholders). There only needs to be one shareholder, so you could hold the company's only share and be its sole owner. Alternatively, all of your family could have a share in the company.

A company must have at least one director which can be the same person as the shareholder. From April 2008, there is no longer a requirement to have a company secretary.

8.1.1. Why is it called a limited company?

One of the non-tax advantages of having a company is that the owners are protected should a claim be made against it. For example, if one of your tenants falls down a step in your property and seriously hurts himself, he may decide to sue you. If you own the property and don't have adequate insurance cover you would be personally liable to pay any damages awarded and could end up losing your own house. If the company owns the property, then you will have more financial protection against any such claims. Your liability as a shareholder is, therefore, limited (hence "limited company") to the money you put into the company.

However, this doesn't mean that if the company takes out a large mortgage to buy a property and there's subsequently a crash in property prices, you can just walk away from the company's debts. This is because banks and other mortgage lenders are very cautious about lending to limited companies and will almost certainly require a personal guarantee from you as the owner. A personal guarantee means that if the company can't pay its mortgage debt, then the bank will come knocking on your door to settle up.

NOTE. Although the shareholders have limited liability, you are also likely to be a director and, by law, it's the directors that are responsible for the actions of the company. You could, therefore, find yourself personally liable for debts or claims if they have arisen directly as a result of your actions or decisions.

8.1.2. How do I set up a limited company?

First, you need to choose a suitable name for a company. You can't have the same name as another company (you can check whether your name is original by visiting the Companies House website at http://www.companieshouse.gov.uk and clicking on "Find Company Information").

Once you have chosen a name, you also need to choose the director (most probably you).

The easiest way to legally set up a company is to use the Business Link/ Companies House Web Incorporation Service which you can access from http://www.companieshouse.gov.uk/infoAndGuide/companyRegistration.shtml.

This service costs £18 and is far cheaper than using a formation agent or accountant who will charge anything up to £300 to set it up for you.

Once the company is set up, you need to set up a company bank account. Certain banks offer free banking for companies with a relatively small number of transactions so shop around and don't automatically set up the account with the bank you use personally.

8.1.3. How much does it cost to run a limited company?

A company needs to pay an annual fee of £40 to Companies House (or £14 if you file the company's annual return online).

It also needs to file statutory accounts with Companies House and it's advisable to get an accountant to prepare these. The fee charged depends on the accountant, but for a simple property investment company with two or three properties, it should be in the region of £500-£1,000 plus VAT a year.

8.2. HOW IS RENTAL INCOME TAXED IN A LIMITED COMPANY?

Instead of income tax, limited companies pay Corporation Tax (CT) on their profits. The rate of tax they pay depends on their level of profits:

Year to 31 March Profits	2012 Tax rate	2013 Tax rate
Up to £300,000	20%	20%
£300,001 to £1,500,000	27.5%	25%
Above £1,500,000	26%	24%

Note. These limits will be reduced if there are associated (under common control) companies.

These lower tax rates are the main reason that investors consider owning properties through a limited company. A higher rate taxpayer would pay 40% on their net rental income and gains. For companies with income and gains under £300,000 a year, the top company tax rate is only 20%.

Example

Jack, a higher rate taxpayer, has rental income of £9,000 a year. If he owned the property personally, he would pay £3,600 in tax on these profits (£9,000 x 40%). However, if the property was owned by a limited company, the company would pay tax of £1,800 (£9,000 x 20%). A very significant tax saving of £1,800 (£9,000 x 20%) on a relatively modest rental income.

Note. Depending on your other income, there may be further tax to pay if the profits are taken out of the company as dividends.

8.3. HOW ARE CAPITAL GAINS TAXED IN A LIMITED COMPANY?

Unlike sole owners and partnerships, a company doesn't pay CGT on any capital gains it makes on the sale of a property - it pays CT instead. Any capital gains are added to the company's rental profits in the year and the company then pays CT at the rates shown in 8.2.

Example

William purchased his property using a limited company. There was a taxable gain of £50,000 when the property was sold several years later.

The company also had rental income of £4,000 in the year the property was sold. So, the company will pay CT on total profits of £54,000. At this level, the rate of tax is 20%, and the company's tax bill will be £10,800 (20% x £54,000).

8.3.1. Can companies still claim indexation relief on their gains?

Yes. Unlike individuals, when it was stopped in April 2008, companies continue to be able to claim indexation relief.

8.3.2. What is indexation relief?

This relief increases the cost of the property to take account of inflation and therefore reduces your gain.

8.3.3. How do I calculate indexation relief?

This relief is based on the percentage increase in the Retail Price Index (RPI) from the date you purchased or acquired the asset up to the date you sell it. You can find the relevant inflation factors from March 1982 at http://www.hmrc.gov.uk/rates/cg-indexation-allowance/index.htm.

The relief is calculated by multiplying the purchase cost of the property by the inflation factor for the month that you bought (or acquired) it.

$$\text{Purchase cost x inflation factor for month of purchase}$$
$$= \text{indexation relief}$$

To find the relevant inflation factor, go to HMRC's indexation allowance tables index (at the above address) and click on the table for the month you disposed of the property. Then find the inflation factor in the table for the month when you purchased the property.

EXAMPLE

B Ltd bought a property in August 2000 for £100,000. It sold it in January 2012 for £180,000. From the January 2012 indexation allowance table, the inflation factor for August 2000 is 0.396. Therefore, B Ltd can reduce its gain by indexation relief of £39,600 (£100,000 x 0.396).

Improvement costs

You can also claim the relief on the costs of any improvements you've made to the property. Check the dates on the receipts to find out which month you incurred the costs, find the inflation factor for that month and then multiply the cost by that inflation factor.

EXAMPLE

Taking the above example, B Ltd spent £10,000 on a loft extension for the property in March 2005. The inflation factor for March 2005 is 0.249. Therefore, B Ltd can further reduce its gain by indexation relief of £2,490 (£10,000 x 0.249).

8.3.4. What happens if the relief is more than the gain?

Indexation relief can only be used to reduce or eliminate a capital gain. This means that the relief can't be more than the gain, i.e. you can't use it to make a capital loss.

EXAMPLE

Taking the first example above, if B Ltd sold the property for £130,000, it has only made a gain before indexation of £30,000. In this case, the maximum amount of indexation relief that it could offset would be £30,000 (and not £39,600).

8.3.5. The company purchased the property before March 31 1982, so what indexation factor do I use?

This relief was introduced in March 1982, so indexation allowances only start from that date. However, if you bought or acquired a property before that date, then the "purchase cost" for the calculation is the higher of the actual purchase cost and its market value at March 31 1982. In practice, if you don't know its market value at that date then you could use the purchase cost. However, using the market value in the calculation will probably save you more tax, as it's likely to be higher than the original cost.

Valuing the property at March 31 1982

It's best to use a chartered surveyor to get a valuation, although you can estimate the value yourself. Either way, it's worth getting the Taxman to agree it before you submit the company's tax return. This will avoid him raising an enquiry and disputing the valuation later (which could lead to the company having to pay interest and maybe even penalties). The easiest way to do this is to use the Taxman's post-transaction valuation check form, CG34, which you can download from http://www.hmrc.gov.uk/forms/cg34.pdf.

Once you send the form in, the Taxman has to come back with an answer within 56 days (his published target) so he's under pressure to make a quick decision.

8.4. HOW DO I TAKE MONEY OUT OF A LIMITED COMPANY?

The company tax rates do seem very favourable compared with the higher income tax rate of 40% for all income over £42,475 for 2012/13. However, you need to bear in mind that the profits must remain in the company to take full advantage of the lower CT rates. If you want to draw money out of the company, you will usually have to pay tax on this at the higher income tax rates. The two most common ways of taking money out of a company are as salary or dividends.

8.4.1. Paying yourself a salary

If you decide to draw money out of the company by paying a salary, then you will have to pay income tax on this if your total income for the year is over £8,105 (2012/13). On top of this, the company will also have to pay 13.8% NI if the salary is more than £144 a week (2012/13) and you will have to pay 12% NI if the salary is over £146 a week (2012/13).

EXAMPLE

Neville needs to withdraw money from his property investment company. He decides to pay himself a salary of £4,000. As Neville receives a salary of £70,000 from his main job, he will be taxed at 40% on this salary (£1,600). Therefore, he will only receive a net salary of £2,400. He won't have to pay NI because the salary is less than £146 per week (£7,605 a year).

The company will also avoid paying 13.8% NI as long as the salary is less than £146 per week. The salary can be offset against the company's profits to reduce its CT bill.

8.4.2. Paying yourself a dividend

One of the most popular methods of taking money out of a company is as a dividend. This is mainly because by paying a dividend, both you and the company avoid paying NI.

The additional advantage is that a dividend carries a tax credit which means that basic rate taxpayers have no additional tax to pay. However, higher rate taxpayers still have to pay an additional tax equal to 25% of the dividend they receive (for additional (50%) rate taxpayers, it's equal to 36.11% of the net dividend).

The disadvantage of dividends is that the company cannot offset them against its profits to reduce the tax bill.

EXAMPLE

Instead of a £4,000 gross salary, Neville decides to take the money out of the company as a dividend. Neville takes a dividend of £3,200 as, after paying the additional 25% tax on the dividend (£32,00 x 25% = £800), Neville is still left with £2,400 in his pocket. He therefore saves £800 in tax by taking a dividend instead of a salary.

However, the company will lose CT relief on the £4,000 salary not taken, which at the small companies rate of 20% would mean additional CT to pay of £800. So overall, paying a dividend to give the same take home pay would mean paying exactly the same amount of tax as paying a salary. However, if the company paid tax at the higher rate of 24%, then, in this example, taking the salary rather than a dividend would be the most tax-effective strategy.

8.4.3.   When is it preferable to take a salary?

Most tax advisors recommend that their clients take dividends rather than salary. However, there are a few situations (as seen in the above example) when it's preferable to take a salary instead.

It would also be very beneficial to pay a salary to someone who doesn't currently have any income (for example, your spouse or child). This is because the salary can be deducted from the company's profits to reduce the CT bill, but the individual won't pay any income tax or NI.

EXAMPLE

Brian pays his non-working wife a salary of £5,000 as she does occasional work for the company. As this is below the personal allowance of £8,105 (2012/13), his wife has no tax to pay. The company can still offset this salary against its profits, saving CT at 20% of £1,000.

8.4.4.   When is it preferable to take a dividend?

If you want to withdraw more than the employers' NI threshold (£7,488 a year (£144 a week) for 2012/13), the company will have to pay 13.8% NI on any salary amount over this limit. In this case, it would be better to take anything over £144 a week as a dividend.

EXAMPLE

Jenny is a higher rate taxpayer and wants to take £8,000 out of the company.

If Jenny takes an £8,000 salary instead, she will have to pay 40% tax on this (£3,200) and 12% NI (assuming she has no other employment income in the year and can't get a deferment to just pay 2%) on the amount over £7,605, i.e. £47 (£8,000 - £7,605 x 12%). Leaving her with net income of £4,753. The company will also have to pay 13.8% NI on the amount over £7,488, £71. But the company will get 20% tax relief on the salary plus the employers' NI, £1,614 (£8,000 + £71 x 20%). An overall tax cost of £1,703.

If, instead, she takes a dividend of £6,337 to leave her with the same net income of £4,753, she will have to pay a further 25% tax on it of £1,584.

Therefore, the saving by taking the dividend is £119 (£1,703 - £1,584).

8.5. ADVANTAGES OF USING A LIMITED COMPANY

As mentioned in 8.2., the main reason that property investors are buying properties through limited companies is the lower tax rates. However, there are other advantages to using a limited company.

Indexation relief

Unlike individuals, a company can still claim indexation relief. This relief increases the purchase cost in line with inflation, therefore reducing the gain.

Stamp Duty Land Tax savings

If you buy shares in a property company, then you will only pay Stamp Duty at 0.5% rather than up to 7% when you purchase a property as an individual.

Limited liability

If the company manages to get a mortgage without your personal guarantee, then your personal assets will be protected should there be a property price crash.

8.6. DISADVANTAGES OF USING A LIMITED COMPANY

As discussed in 8.3., one of the main disadvantages of having a limited company is that there could be a further tax charge should you wish to extract any of the proceeds from the company.

There are also other tax disadvantages:

No annual CGT allowance

Unlike sole owners and partnerships, companies cannot use the annual CGT allowance (£10,600 for 2012/13). This means that if you and your spouse jointly owned a property, you would lose out on a combined CGT allowance of £21,200 if the property was held in a company. At the 20% small company tax rate that's extra tax of £4,240.

No principal private residence relief

You cannot claim principal private residence relief or private letting relief when the properties are held in a limited company. Chapter 5 showed how important these reliefs could be in reducing, or even eliminating, the capital gain.

CT rate may be higher than the CGT rate

The lowest rate of CT is 20% but the lowest rate of CGT is 18%, so you could be paying at least 2% more on any gains. However, you can claim indexation relief (see 8.3.1).

CGT when you transfer a property into a limited company

If you want to move a property into a limited company, then it must be transferred at market value. If the market value is more than what you originally paid for the property, then this could trigger an immediate CGT liability.

Increased administration costs

Accountants will usually charge more for preparing limited company accounts (usually at least double what you pay to have sole trader accounts drawn up).

Fewer finance choices

Lenders are often less willing to lend to limited companies so there will be less choice for you when choosing a mortgage and the rates may well be higher.

15% Stamp Duty Land Tax (SDLT) on residential properties costing more than £2 million for purchases from March 21 2012

The Budget 2012 announced that if a residential property worth over £2 million is purchased by a company, then the company faces a SDLT charge of 15%. This 15% charge is 8% higher than the new 7% SDLT rate for residential properties over £2 million purchased by individuals. The Budget 2012 also announced that the government plans to consult on a possible annual charge for companies which already hold £2 million plus residential properties which would come into effect sometime in 2013.

Buying strategies to avoid tax

8.7. SO SHOULD I BUY A RESIDENTIAL PROPERTY THROUGH A LIMITED COMPANY?

The decision as to whether to own a property through a limited company depends on a number of factors:

- do you already run a business through your own company?
- how many similar properties do you want to purchase in the future?
- will the properties cost more than £2 million?
- when do you intend to sell the property?

8.7.1. I already have a company

If you already run your business through a company it's normally more tax efficient to own the property personally.

This will enable you use your CGT annual exemption (and your spouse's annual exemption if the property is jointly owned).

The net rental income generated will be taxed at your top rate of tax (i.e. 40% for a higher rate taxpayer), but if you have a large mortgage on the property, it's likely that your income tax bill will be relatively small.

There are also other factors to consider:

Loss of entrepreneurs' relief

If you already have your own company and you want to use it to buy a residential property, then you may find that the company fails to qualify as a trading company. This will mean that you won't be able to claim entrepreneurs' relief (see 9.2.) when you sell your shares in the company.

Associated company problems

If you form a new company to buy the residential property and you own more than 50% of the shares in each one, you may find that you end up with a higher CT bill on your trading company. This is because (unless you make more than £1,500,000 of taxable profits) the two companies will be regarded as being "associated". When two companies are associated, the CT thresholds are halved. This means that it is only the first £150,000 of each company's profits that would be taxed at 20%. Even if you control one company and your spouse controls the other, the companies will be considered to be associated.

8.7.2. I don't already have a company

Personal or joint ownership may still be the more appropriate route due to the availability of the CGT annual exemption and the lower CGT rate being lower than company rates. However, if you are likely to be reinvesting the company's profits (rather than drawing money out of the company) to buy more residential properties then it may be beneficial to set up a limited company.

EXAMPLE

Simone owns three properties in her own name and she receives rental income of £16,000 a year from these properties. As a higher rate taxpayer, Simone will pay £6,400 leaving her with a net £9,600 to invest in her next property.

If Simone owned the same three properties in her limited company, Simone Properties Ltd, then the company would pay just £3,200 in tax. This would leave the company with £12,800 to invest in the next property. An extra £3,200.

NOTE. Although you can reinvest the profits, it's likely that at some point you will want to withdraw money from the company. Whenever you do this, you will be liable to the double tax charge - the company paying CT on the profits and you paying income tax on either the salary or dividend (but see 8.7.3.).

8.7.3. The tax advantages of long-term investment

There are potential long-term advantages of owning residential property in a company which counteracts the loss of the CGT exemption. These methods only work if you intend to keep the properties for a number of years.

Continue to rent the properties in the company as a retirement fund

If you intend to keep the properties for many years, then you could consider the property investment company as a "retirement fund". If the properties are retained into retirement, it's likely that any initial financing of the purchase of the property has been paid off and there will be a strong income stream. The profits of the company (after paying CT) can be paid out to you and/or your spouse as shareholder dividends.

To the extent that the dividends when added to your other income do not exceed your personal allowances and the starting and basic rate bands (£42,475 for 2012/13), you will have no income tax to pay.

Sell the properties and use the company as a retirement fund

This scheme works as long as you are happy to leave the rental income in the company to accumulate for a number of years.

As you know, if the rental income in your company is less than £300,000 a year then there is just 20% tax to pay as long as you don't take the income out as dividends. So, the after-tax rental profits are kept in the company until you wish to retire in, say, ten years' time.

Just before your retirement, you sell all the properties in the company. Unlike for individuals, this will only trigger a CGT liability if the property values have increased by more than inflation due to the company being able to claim indexation relief.

You now need to get the money out of the company. If you wind it up to extract the funds as a capital distribution, then you'll have quite a large CGT bill (investment companies are not entitled to entrepreneurs' relief, so the rate would be 28%).

However, you could take dividends for a number of years instead (keeping your total income under £42,475 each year) without paying any tax. Once you've taken most of the profits out as dividends, you can leave up to £10,600 (based on 2012/13 tax rates) in the company to cover your CGT annual allowance). You can liquidate the company without paying CGT.

By doing this, you have paid just 20% on your rental profits and avoided any tax on taking the money out of the company.

Selling the shares instead of the property

You will pay CGT on any increase in the share value over your CGT annual allowance at a rate of 18% or 28% depending on your total income for the year. If you will pay tax on the gain at 18%, then there would be an advantage to selling the shares instead of the property if you would have had to pay 25% tax on any dividends you took out to get the sales proceeds into your own hands.

This may also be more attractive to the purchaser of the properties rather than buying the properties directly, as they will only have 0.5% Stamp Duty Land Tax to pay rather than the potentially higher sums (1% to 7%) of Stamp Duty Land Tax on the property purchases.

8.8. USING A PROPERTY MANAGEMENT COMPANY

If you've decided that it's desirable to hold the properties personally, you could still make use of the lower company tax rates by using a property management company.

8.8.1. What is a property management company?

A property management company is one that is set up to manage your property portfolio. However, the properties are still owned by you personally and not the company. Effectively, the management company acts as a letting agent.

The company would provide the usual letting agent services such as ongoing maintenance, repairs and property inspections. The company would be set up as in 8.1.2.

8.8.2. How will a property management company save me tax?

As mentioned in 8.2., companies pay a lower rate of tax than individuals. The tax savings are best shown by way of example:

EXAMPLE

Lucy has a salary of £40,000 per year making her a higher rate taxpayer. She also owns three properties which give her rental income of £30,000 and profits after deducting mortgage interest and other allowable expenses of £15,000 a year. Therefore, she pays £6,000 (40% of £15,000) in tax on the rental profits.

Lucy decides to set up a property management company to manage the properties. The company charges Lucy 15% of the rental income, £375 per month to manage the properties. This means that Lucy is paying the £4,500 a year rental profits into the company as management fees.

Lucy can deduct these management fees from her rental profits so her rental profits are reduced to £10,500 and she has a reduced tax bill of £4,200. The company has tax to pay at 20% on its profits, i.e. £900 (£4,500 x 20%). Lucy, therefore, makes an overall tax saving of £900 a year by having a property management company (providing she keeps the profits in the company and doesn't withdraw them as dividends).

NOTE. If you already have a trading company and set up another company to act as the property management company, the two will be classed as associated and the 21% tax limit will be halved to £150,000 (see 8.7.1.) for each company.

TIP 1

It would be advisable to leave the money in the company if you're a higher rate taxpayer, otherwise you'll end up paying 25% tax on the dividend taken out. After one year, if you liquidate the company, you can claim entrepreneurs' relief (property management is a trade) and only pay CGT on the money at 10%. Alternatively, if your spouse has little or no income, make sure they are the sole shareholder in your company so they can take the dividend out tax-free.

Tip 2

If you're a basic rate taxpayer, then it's not worth setting up a property management company as the lowest company tax rate is the same as the basic tax rate, i.e. 20%. Therefore, you won't make any tax savings but you'll still have to pay the increased administration costs of a limited company.

8.8.3. How much can the property management company charge?

The charges must be at a commercial rate. If you only have one property, the Taxman won't let you get away with charging £375 a month. Commercial letting agents usually charge around 10%-15% of the gross rental income for a full management service. Therefore, if you rent out a property for £600 a month, then the company can charge you £90 a month (15% of £600) as a management fee.

8.8.4. Does there need to be a formal contract between me and the company?

In order to avoid a challenge from the Taxman, yes. The contract should outline the management services that the company is providing to you such as:

- finding new tenants
- issuing tenancy agreements
- maintenance and upkeep of the properties
- resolving tenant queries.

The contract should also state the monthly charge (either as a fixed figure or as a percentage of the gross rental income).

See Appendix F for a sample contract.

8.8.5. Should I set up a property management company?

If you are a property investor and:

- you don't already have a limited company
- you are a higher rate taxpayer
- your rental profits are at least £5,000 a year
- you can afford to leave the money in the company or are able to pay dividends to someone who only pays basic rate tax

---

then you will save tax by using a property management company. The rental profits should be above £5,000 in order that the tax saving (£1,000 for a higher rate taxpayer) is not wiped out by the additional cost of running a limited company (see 8.1.3.). But remember you will need to leave the money in the company or you'll pay another 25% tax on any dividend taken out.

8.8.6. VAT and property management companies

Property management services are standard-rated for VAT so a property management business will need to be registered for VAT if its annual turnover exceeds the VAT registration threshold (£77,000 from April 2012). You can still register for VAT voluntarily if the company's income is under this threshold.

If you do register for VAT, you can reclaim VAT on your management company expenses, e.g. accountancy fees.

9. Investing in commercial property

9.1. WHY SHOULD I INVEST IN COMMERCIAL PROPERTY?

Most people choose to invest in residential properties such as houses and flats, which can be rented out relatively easily and, when looking at the long term, provide excellent capital growth. However, investors have realised that commercial properties such as shops and offices can also provide a good return on the original investment. With commercial property, generally the emphasis is on income – a higher income than residential property, albeit generally with a lower rate of capital growth. Below are a number of other advantages:

- commercial leases are contractual as opposed to the statutory regulated ones for residential. This means that generally the landlord/investor has more protection if the tenant fails to pay rent or meet their contract commitments

- the Full Repairing and Insuring (FRI) lease agreement is accepted as the norm for commercial tenancies in the UK. This means that the tenant is responsible for repairs, renovations and insurance so the landlord can expect a clear return on their investment, free from any additional costs

- leases are agreed for much longer periods than the common six-month tenancy agreement on a flat or house. Five, ten or even 15 years would not be unusual with a commercial tenancy, so generally there's a lot less management involvement needed from the landlord or their agent and there is a guaranteed income for a number of years.

Prior to April 2008, the Capital Gains Tax (CGT) regime made personal investment in commercial property much more favourable than investing in residential properties. One of the main reasons for this was a very generous business asset taper relief which cut the gain by 75% after two years. However, since April 6 2008 business asset taper relief has been replaced with entrepreneurs' relief (see 9.2.) and most commercial properties do not qualify for this.

9.2. CAN I TAKE ADVANTAGE OF ENTREPRENEURS' RELIEF?

Any gains made on the disposal of commercial properties are taxed the same rate as residential properties, i.e. 18% or 28% depending on your total income for the year.

There is, however, a relief available (entrepreneurs' relief) which can reduce the tax rate to 10% but, unfortunately, very few commercial properties will qualify for this.

9.2.1. What is entrepreneurs' relief?

With regards to commercial property sales, entrepreneurs' relief (ER) is only available to you if you used it in your own business or if you are a qualifying company shareholder or partner in a partnership and own the premises from which the company/partnership trades. As long as you sell the premises: (i) within three years of selling your business; or (ii) at the same time as you sell your shares in your personal company or your partnership share (an associated disposal), any gain will qualify for ER meaning that you only pay 10% tax on the gain.

However, if you have charged a market rent to your business for use of the premises, then it will not qualify for ER and you will pay up to 28% tax on the gain. Where you received rent at less than market value, there will be a partial restriction to ER.

NOTE. There is a £10 million lifetime limit on the gains that qualify for ER.

9.2.2. Do furnished holiday homes qualify for entrepreneurs' relief?

As long as certain criteria are met (see 3.2.), as discussed in 6.2.8., "furnished holiday accommodation" is treated as a trade and therefore the disposal of the property will be treated as a disposal of the business and should qualify for ER.

9.3. SHOULD MY COMPANY'S PREMISES BE OWNED BY ME OR THE COMPANY?

In the past, it was almost always better to own your business premises personally and rent it to your trading company due to the very beneficial business asset taper relief. But now that company tax rates (20% or 24%) are lower than the CGT tax rate that you're likely to pay when you dispose of a property (28%), it may not be so advantageous to do so.

However, there are still the following tax advantages to owning the business premises personally:

- the rent you receive from the company allows profit to be extracted without having to pay NI
- the rent is a tax-deductible expense for the company
- if you take out a mortgage on the property, you can offset the interest against the rent (and it may be easier to get a mortgage personally)

- as you own it personally, you (and your spouse if it is owned jointly) will be entitled to the CGT annual exemption (£10,600 each for 2012/13)

- if you don't charge a market rent, you should be entitled to ER meaning that the capital gain will be taxed at 10% rather than 28%

- when you sell the property, you will receive the sale proceeds personally, therefore avoiding the double tax problem when trying to draw money out of the company.

> **TIP**
>
> If you do own your company premises in the company, you could sell the shares in that company, instead of (for example) the company selling the property and then deciding whether to continue with the company or wind it up. It may also be attractive for a purchaser to buy the shares in a property company, rather than buy the property directly as they will pay only 0.5% Stamp Duty instead of up to 7%. Your share disposal should also qualify for ER as long as it's a trading company so you could end up only paying 10% CGT up to the £10 million lifetime limit.

NOTE. If you do own the property personally and charge rent to the company, then you will not be able to claim the 10% CGT rate when you sell the property even if you sell it as part of the sale of the business so you need to weigh up the extra 18% CGT you may pay on the sale against the advantages of owning it personally.

9.3.1. Do I need a formal letting agreement between me and my company?

Yes, the rent should normally be paid under a formal agreement between you and the company. This agreement will set out how often the rent should be paid, either monthly, quarterly or annually. See Appendix G for a specimen licence agreement.

9.3.2. Tax-avoidance strategy: use a licence instead of a lease

Problem

As discussed in more detail in 10.3., Stamp Duty Land Tax (SDLT) is due on the grant of a lease. The SDLT payable on the grant of a lease is based on the net present value (i.e. the value in today's money) of all the rent payable under the lease over its full term. For commercial property, where the net present value (NPV) is more than £150,000, SDLT is due at the rate of 1% on the excess. So if you decide to rent a property to your company, it would have to pay SDLT on any lease agreement with a net present value over £150,000 (visit http://ldccalculator. hmrc.gov.uk/LDC01.aspx to work out the net present value).

EXAMPLE

Mr Austin owns a warehouse, which is occupied by his company, Austin Enterprises Ltd. Mr Austin wants to charge the company a rent so he can get money out of it without paying NI. If he grants the company a 20-year lease on June 1 2012 at an annual market rent of £30,000 per year, the adjusted NPV is £426,371 and SDLT of £2,763 is payable (£426,371 - £150,000 exempt = £276,371 x 1% SDLT rate).

If you let your company occupy your premises in return for a rent, the Taxman could argue that you have granted a lease even where there is no paperwork to prove that you have done so. If he treats it as a lease, then he could seek to collect the overdue SDLT plus interest and penalties.

Solution

One way that family companies can avoid SDLT is to use a licence to occupy instead of a lease. What's the difference? Put simply, a lease is a contract which gives the tenant exclusive possession for a period of time. On the other hand, a licence is a personal right to occupy property on a non-exclusive basis. The main differences are:

- a licence cannot be sold or given away whereas a lease can be assigned to someone else

- a lessor cannot enter the property whereas a licensor can.

Action

Speak to your solicitor and ask him to consider drawing up a licence instead of a lease.

9.3.3. How much rent should I charge?

A little?

You can charge the company as little rent as you wish for using your property. However, if the rent is not enough to cover the expenses connected with the property, such as loan interest, you will lose money. Any loss you make from letting property can only be offset against profits from letting in the future; it cannot be used to reduce tax due on your other income in the same or earlier years.

A lot?

If the company pays you a very high rent (above the market rate), the Taxman may argue that the excess is actually a disguised form of salary and will insist that this excess is taxed like a salary.

Ideally, you want to charge a rent that will just cover the property expenses, such as repairs, insurance and mortgage interest. Charging any more could mean that the rent is taxed at a higher rate in your hands than the profits would be taxed if they remained in the company. For example, the company may save Corporation Tax at 20% by paying you rent. You would then have to pay tax at your highest rate of 40% on any rent received that is not offset by the property expenses.

9.3.4. Do I have to charge VAT on the rent?

Not registered for VAT

You don't charge VAT on top of the rent you charge the company. However, you might end up with some irrecoverable input VAT suffered on the cost of acquiring the building originally and/or refurbishing it. The rule is, "no VAT charge, no VAT recovery!".

Registered for VAT

As the building is used for commercial purposes (i.e. not a residential property), you can register for VAT and opt to tax it. This means that you would charge VAT on the rent. However, you are now able to recover all the VAT on your costs. Of course, this means completing a VAT return and paying any VAT you owe.

9.3.5. So, should I register for VAT?

If you've been charged substantial VAT on acquiring the building or incur significant VAT on expenditure to it (e.g. during a refurbishment) then register for VAT and opt to tax and recover the VAT now. Assuming your company is also VAT-registered, it will be able to recover the VAT you charge it and you can also reclaim the VAT that you incurred.

If the company makes exempt supplies, (e.g. an insurance company), then it won't be able to reclaim the VAT you would have to charge on the rent so it may be better for you not to register for VAT. However, if you had to pay a large amount of input VAT on the purchase of the property, then there will still be a cash-flow advantage in registering as you can claim all the VAT back on the purchase immediately.

If you haven't been charged VAT on acquiring the building and your VAT costs are small, then don't bother to opt to tax. The additional administration costs of completing quarterly VAT returns will outweigh any small VAT savings.

WARNING! You cannot change your option to tax the property once it has been exercised for 20 years. Therefore, if your company changes from being standard-rated to exempt for VAT, you will need to charge VAT even if the company cannot recover it.

How do I opt to tax?

You can opt to tax by writing to HM Revenue & Customs and giving details of the property you want to opt. It's best to use Form VAT 1614 which can be downloaded from http://www.hmrc.gov.uk/forms/vat1614a.pdf. You need to notify HMRC within 30 days of opting.

TIP

It's important to establish that HMRC have received your notification to opt. Therefore, send in a duplicate notification for stamping and return by HMRC.

WARNING! Always seek professional advice before opting to tax a property. Getting the decision wrong could prove to be very costly.

9.3.6.   Tax-avoidance strategy: register for VAT then de-register

Problem

You privately own a commercial property that you rent out. You have not exercised the option to tax because the property is occupied by a tenant (e.g. your company) which is either exempt or unregistered for VAT, i.e. they could not reclaim any of the VAT you would have to charge on rent if you were registered. As you're not VAT registered, you can't reclaim the VAT on any major maintenance work (e.g. significant roof repairs) done on the property.

Solution

Register for VAT and opt to tax the property. This way you can recover all of the input VAT on your major maintenance work. This must be done in advance of any work being started so that all the bills arrive after the VAT registration.

Remember that you will need to charge VAT on any rent charged to your tenant while you are VAT registered.

Once the work has been completed, de-register. You can voluntarily de-register because you are trading below the VAT limits (you no longer have to wait a year before de-registering). The deregistration limit from April 2012 is £75,000.

Does the VATman really allow this?

On de-registration, you normally have to pay back the VAT on relevant assets where the VAT comes to more than £1,000. However, this only applies to goods not services.

Building work is classed as a service so is not caught by this provision. Providing the building work is just repairs, and not improvements, then it won't be classed as an asset either.

NOTE. Even though you've de-registered for VAT, the option to tax will still apply for 20 years. This means that if you sell the building for more than the registration threshold during this period you will have to re-register for VAT. However, if there is a sitting tenant in the property, it should be treated as a "transfer of a going concern" and no VAT will be chargeable anyway.

9.4. TAX-AVOIDANCE STRATEGY: USE A PENSION SCHEME TO BUY A COMMERCIAL PROPERTY

Rather than owning the property personally, you could set up a personal pension scheme which could own the property. The scheme could then lease the property back to your business.

The advantage of a pension scheme is that its income is tax-free so it wouldn't have to pay tax on the rent it receives from your company. Also, if you later sell the property in the pension scheme, you avoid paying CGT on any gain made.

Additionally, because all pensions are written in trust, your fund is not classed as part of your estate for Inheritance Tax purposes if you die before retirement.

9.4.1. How do I set up a pension scheme?

You need to speak to an Independent Financial Adviser (IFA) about your company setting up a Self-Invested Personal Pension (SIPP) and possibly transferring your current pension fund into it. A SIPP is basically the same as any other personal pension plan except that you have more control over what your contributions are invested in and one of the main attractions of a SIPP is that it can be used to purchase commercial property. This is enhanced by the fact that the Taxman will allow such a property to be leased back to your business. Therefore, you get a double benefit as the commercial property is being used both to help your business and provide for your future financial security.

EXAMPLE

Tim has a company which is looking for new business premises. He has already accumulated £100,000 within his pension arrangements. A suitable property will cost £150,000. He has been advised that he could purchase a property by using a SIPP. The £100,000 already in his pension fund could be used as a deposit with the SIPP borrowing the remaining £50,000. (A SIPP can borrow up to 50% of the scheme's assets before the borrowing has taken place).

Tim's company would then be able to trade from the new property and pay a fair rent to the pension fund. The company will be able to offset this rent against its profits for tax purposes. The pension fund, however, would not have to pay tax on the rent or any capital gains should the property increase in value.

From Tim's point of view, although the property will assist him in building his business, it is also helping him build up his pension assets. Significantly, as the property is held within the pension fund, it would normally be creditor proof, should the company run into financial difficulties.

9.4.2. How much can a SIPP borrow to buy a commercial property?

Prior to "A" day (April 6 2006), a SIPP could borrow up to 75% of a commercial property's purchase price. So, if your pension fund was worth £100,000, then you could have bought a property worth up to £400,000.

However, since April 2006, you are only able to borrow 50% of the fund's value. In this case, if your pension fund is worth £100,000, you can only buy a property worth up to £150,000.

9.4.3. What other benefits does a SIPP offer?

The flexibility of investment in a SIPP is not just limited to commercial property. You can also make direct investments in stocks and shares. This avoids you being locked into a poorly performing investment fund. As the SIPP enjoys all the tax advantages of an ordinary personal pension you can also switch to a new fund without paying any CGT.

9.4.4. What are the disadvantages of a SIPP?

The main disadvantage is centred around the fact that because a SIPP is a bespoke solution rather than an off-the-shelf product, the costs are higher.

9.4.5. Would I benefit from setting up a SIPP?

Due to the higher costs, you would only really benefit from a SIPP if you already have a reasonably large pension fund, say over £100,000, which you could transfer into it.

9.5. CAPITAL ALLOWANCES

The types of expenditure that you can claim against your commercial property rental income are much the same as for residential accommodation. The one major difference is that, unlike residential property (see 2.6.), if you own a commercial property (including furnished holiday accommodation), you can claim capital allowances on any fixtures and fittings that you purchase for use in the property. This compensates for the fact that you can't claim wear and tear allowance on commercial property rentals.

9.5.1. What are the capital allowance rates?

The rates for 2012/13 are the same as those shown in section 2.6. So, as a small business, you can claim 100% of the first £25,000 spent on qualifying assets such as fixtures, fittings and equipment in each tax year. You can claim just 8% or 18% (depending on the type of asset) on any expenditure over £25,000 in the year you buy the assets and then 8% or 18% on the unrelieved balance of this expenditure in subsequent years.

9.5.2. How to claim 100% of the cost of equipment purchases over £25,000 against your rental income

As mentioned in 9.5.1., you can claim 100% of the first £25,000 you spend on qualifiying assets for your commercial property. But on top of this, if you invest in energy or water-saving equipment, you can also claim 100% of their costs against your rental income in the year of purchase. This could include an energy-efficient boiler or water-efficient taps. The full technology and product lists can be seen at http://etl.decc.gov.uk/.

9.5.3. Can I claim capital allowances on the fixtures present when I buy the property?

Pre-April 2012, if you bought a commercial building - whether to trade from yourself or let out - you were free to identify plant and equipment that were contained within it, such as heating and lighting, air conditioning and ventilation systems, lifts, carpets, security systems, sanitaryware etc., which qualified for capital allowances but which the previous owner had overlooked. You could then apportion a "just and reasonable" part of the purchase cost of the building to equipment, and use this as a basis to make a substantial capital allowances claim.

However, for equipment on which the previous owner had claimed capital allowances, you could come to an agreement with the seller to fix its value by means of a joint tax election (known as a s.198 election).

This often set up a conflict between the seller, who would want to attribute a low value to the assets (to maximise the capital allowances they can claim), and the buyer, who would want a high value because they could then claim capital allowances on this amount (and save Stamp Duty Land Tax - see 10.2). Importantly, this left the buyer open to identify assets not covered by the election and on which they could claim capital allowances.

Changes from April 2012

From April 1 2012 for companies and April 6 2012 for individuals and partnerships, the principle is broadly that, within two years of completion of the sale, the buyer and seller can either:

- make an election, which fixes the value for capital allowances for both parties at an amount which can't exceed a just and reasonable sum; or
- in the absence of an election, e.g. where agreement on value can't be reached, refer the valuation to the tax tribunal.

TRAP 1. Failure to take one of these courses of action within the two-year time limit will mean the buyer, and subsequent owners of the property, will lose the right to claim capital allowances on any of the qualifying assets.

TRAP 2. The trouble with the new system is that if you identify an asset on which the seller has overlooked claiming capital allowances, you must alert them to this so that it can be included in an election or referred to the tribunal. Consequently, the chance for buyers to squeeze extra capital allowances from a property purchase has been somewhat reduced - which is precisely what the Taxman had in mind when he drafted the new rules.

TIP

Despite this, if you're buying a commercial property it will still often benefit you to ask a capital allowances expert (if your accountant isn't one, they'll probably know someone who is) to identify and assess the value of qualifying assets in the building. If your expert spots assets the current owner hasn't claimed on, this might be the basis on which to negotiate down the price of the property.

9.5.4.   How do I come to an agreement with the seller?

As mentioned in 9.5.3, you and the seller can decide between yourselves how much of the consideration is to be allocated to fixtures (but not moveable plant) as long as it doesn't exceed a "just and reasonable" amount.

However, there are several conditions:

- the seller must have been claiming capital allowances on the fixtures (therefore, if the seller hadn't previously identified the qualifying plant until the negotiations started, they will need to make a claim before the transfer)
- both you and the seller must lodge a joint election with the Taxman showing how much consideration is to be allocated to the fixtures. The election must be made in writing within two years of the purchase and is irrevocable
- a copy of the election needs to be included with each party's tax return for the period in which the purchase takes place
- the value cannot exceed the original cost to the seller.

The election needs to contain the following information:

- the amount apportioned to each fixture and the total fixed by the election
- the name of each person making the election
- information sufficient to identify each fixture and the relevant property
- details of the interest acquired by the purchaser
- the tax district references of each person making the election.

See Appendix H for sample wording for the joint election.

10. Other tax considerations when buying an investment property

10.1. SHOULD I TAKE OUT AN INTEREST-ONLY OR A REPAYMENT MORTGAGE?

As discussed in 2.2., any interest paid on a loan that is used exclusively for your rental property is tax deductible. However, the amount of tax relief you get depends on the type of loan you take out. Most property investors will finance the purchase of a property with either an interest-only or repayment mortgage. But which is the cheaper option?

EXAMPLE

Repayment mortgage:

With a £100,000 property, on which you paid a deposit of £20,000, you have a ten-year repayment mortgage of £80,400 (that's £80,000 plus £400 for fees). Assuming a fixed rate of 6.35%, the interest cost in the first year would be £4,934.29 with capital repayments of £5,947.31, making a total payment of £10,881.60. In year two, the total payment is the same but the interest element has dropped to £4,545.45 and the repayment has increased to £6,336.15. This means less interest to claim against your rental income and so, assuming you're a higher rate taxpayer, your tax bill increases by £155.54 (40% x (£4,934.29 -£4,545.45)). This may not seem like a lot but over the ten-year term adds up to about £9,000 in additional tax!

Interest-only mortgage:

If the same loan were on interest-only terms (i.e. no loan repayments), the annual interest cost would be the same over the ten years. In our example, that's £5,105.40 p.a., a total of £51,054 over the life of the loan. This means £5,105.40 to deduct from your rental income each year. The difference in tax is shown in the table below.

YEAR	REPAYMENT LOAN (£)	INTEREST-ONLY LOAN (£)	DIFFERENCE (£)	TAX SAVED AT 40% (£)
1	4,934.29	5,105.40	171.11	68.44
2	4,545.45	5,105.40	559.95	223.98
3	4,131.18	5,105.40	974.22	389.69
4	4,689.83	5,105.40	1,415.57	566.23
5	3,219.63	5,105.40	1,885.77	754.31
6	2,718.68	5,105.40	2,386.72	954.69
7	2,184.98	5,105.40	2,920.42	1,168.17
8	1,616.38	5,105.40	3,489.02	1,395.61
9	1,010.61	5,105.40	4,094.79	1,637.92

Year	Repayment Loan (£)	Interest-only Loan (£)	Difference (£)	Tax saved at 40% (£)
10	364.78	5,105.40	4,740.62	1,896.25
Total	**28,415.81**	**51,054.00**	**22,638.19**	**9,055.29**

Table showing the difference in tax between an interest-only mortgage and a repayment mortgage.

As you can see, an interest-only mortgage means a lower tax bill. Also, although you may pay more interest with a repayment mortgage, the overall monthly payments are lower and you could use the additional funds to your advantage.

TIP

If you've got a mortgage on your own home then take out an interest-only loan to purchase a new rental property. Then out of the rents earned, re-direct the extra you would have paid on a repayment mortgage against your residential mortgage. This way you will pay less interest on your residential mortgage, which is not tax-deductible, and more interest on the buy-to-let mortgage, which is tax-deductible.

10.2. STAMP DUTY LAND TAX (SDLT)

From December 1 2003, you have to pay Stamp Duty Land Tax (SDLT) when you purchase a property over a certain price threshold. The new tax is similar to the old Stamp Duty although there are some new rules for payment. SDLT is calculated as a percentage of the purchase price of the property and is paid by the purchaser.

10.2.1. Do I still have to pay SDLT if I'm not resident in the UK?

Unfortunately, yes. SDLT is payable whether or not the purchaser (or seller) is resident in the UK.

10.2.2. What are the rates of SDLT?

From March 22 2012, the rates are:

PURCHASE PRICE	STAMP DUTY (ON THE ENTIRE PROPERTY COST)
Residential property up to £125,000*	0%
Commercial property up to £150,000	0%
Residential property from £125,001 to £250,000	1%
Commercial property from £150,001 to £250,000	1%

Purchase price	Stamp Duty (on the entire property cost)
All property from £250,001 to £500,000	3%
Residential property from £500,000 to £1 million	4%
Commercial property over £500,000	4%
Residential property from £1 million to £2 million	5%
Residential property over £2 million	7%
Residential property over £2 million purchased by certain "non-natural" persons, e.g. companies	15%

* £150,000 if in a disadvantaged area.

Apart from the new 15% rate for properties over £2 million bought by companies, the rate of SDLT remains the same whether you are an individual, partnership, company or trust.

As you can see, a small difference in the purchase price can make a huge difference to the amount of SDLT you pay.

EXAMPLE

Paul wants to make an offer on a property of £251,000. If he purchases the property at this price then the SDLT rate on this property will be 3% and he will therefore have to pay an additional £7,530.

If, however, Paul offers £250,000 for the property, he will only pay SDLT at 1%, which would be £2,500. In this case, a purchase price difference of £1,000, gives rise to an additional £5,030 in SDLT.

10.2.3 SDLT and transfers to connected persons

Generally, there is no "market value" rule for SDLT so the tax is only payable on the actual purchase price of the property.

Transfers to connected companies

There is an exception to the market value rule for transfers to connected companies. In this case, SDLT is payable on the market value of the property on the date it is transferred.

Transfers to spouses

Unlike Capital Gains Tax and Inheritance Tax, there is no SDLT exemption for transfers between spouses/civil partners. However, the "market value" rule does not apply so there will be no SDLT due unless there is some consideration for the purchase. Therefore, if there is no mortgage on the property and it is being gifted to someone else (other than a company) then there will be no SDLT to pay.

NOTE. If a mortgage is being transferred with the property and the balance being transferred is more than £125,00, then this is treated as consideration for SDLT purposes and there will be SDLT to pay.

EXAMPLE

Shirley gifts a house to her civil partner, Kelly. There is a £260,000 mortgage on the property so SDLT of £7,800 (£260,000 x 3%) will be due on the transfer even though there is no consideration.

In this case, it would be sensible for £10,000 to be paid off the mortgage before the transfer is made as this reduces the SDLT bill to £2,500 - a saving of £5,300.

10.2.4. SDLT-avoidance strategy: pay separately for fixtures and fittings

As we've seen, once the price passes the £250,000 threshold, the amount of SDLT due jumps from 1% to 3%, so it doesn't take mathematical genius to work out that you'd be better off buying at or below £250,000.

The seller, on the other hand, doesn't have to pay SDLT, so will want to get as much as possible for their property.

The solution would be for both you and the seller to come to an agreement whereby the seller prices the property at or below £250,000 and you pay separately for any furnishings or fittings.

EXAMPLE

Andy wishes to purchase a house for £255,000. He offers the vendor £250,000 for the house and £5,000 for the carpets, curtains, light fittings, fridge and washing machine. The SDLT he has to pay will be £2,500. If he hadn't paid for the furnishings and fittings separately he would have paid £7,650. He has therefore saved himself £5,150 in SDLT.

Pricing below the £250,000 threshold is, of course, legal, as is negotiating a deal with the seller for furnishings and fittings that takes the actual price paid above £250,000.

However, one of the differences between SDLT and the old stamp duty is that buyers now face the possibility of an enquiry from the Taxman. This is particularly likely when buying properties at a threshold (known as a "pinch point") where the higher rates of tax apply. If you're in these zones, make sure you can back up any separate figure you paid for furnishings and fittings. The amount you pay for furnishings and fittings should be a reasonable market value. If you've paid well over the odds, then the Taxman may well question it it (he has nine months after the return is filed to open an enquiry).

What counts as furnishings and fittings?

The recent case of **Gill Osman v HMRC** involved this exact SDLT avoidance strategy. Gill Osman (GO) decided that the £258,000 purchase price was not just for the property, but that £8,000 was for household items, so-called chattels, on which SDLT isn't payable. GO had spent a good deal of time and effort in valuing the chattels by comparing them to how much she would have had to pay for similar second-hand items. And even before the case got to tribunal the Taxman conceded that she was right about most of these (£7,200 to be exact). However, the remaining £800 was for garage worktops, cupboards and garage door motor and the tribunal found that these weren't chattels, but were part of the building. This meant that the purchase price for the building was £250,800 and, therefore, GO had to pay a further £5,024 in Stamp Duty (£250,800 x 3% - £2,500 already paid).

> **TIP**
>
> As a rough guide, anything moveable is generally not considered to be part of the property, and so is not subject to SDLT.

When decding what is a chattel, the courts will consider two factors:

- how permanently an item is fixed to a property and the extent of the likely damage caused by removing it; and

- whether the item was intended to enhance the property or to be used or enjoyed in its own right.

So, if you paid extra for plants in pots, that would be outside SDLT. However, if they were planted in the ground, they would not be moveable and would therefore be considered part of the property.

You could also pay separately for carpets, curtains, light fittings, fridges, washing machines, garden furniture and ornaments.

10.2.5. How do I pay the SDLT?

You pay the SDLT to your solicitor before you complete the property purchase who then forwards it on to the Taxman. Although it's ultimately your responsibility, your solicitor will also complete the self-assessment land transaction return for you (although you have to sign it). This has to be submitted to the Taxman within 30 days of the completion date and you, not your solicitor, will be liable to a £100 fine if it's late by less than three months and £200 if more than three months late.

10.2.6. SDLT savings when buying a property in a "disadvantaged" area

However, properties in certain areas of the country are exempt from SDLT.

In these so-called "disadvantaged" areas, the exemption relates to residential properties purchased for less than £150,000.

Which areas are exempt?

There is an interactive disadvantaged area search tool on the Taxman's website, http://www.hmrc.gov.uk/so/dar/dar-search.htm. Just enter the postcode of the property you wish to buy and it will tell you whether it's a deprived area or not. You may be surprised by the areas that are classed as deprived - even parts of Kensington and Chelsea qualify!

WARNING! On his website, the Taxman has relied on postcode data for identifying exempt areas. But there is a time lag between a new postcode being created - for example, when a new development is built - and it being included on the Taxman's website. An estimated 8,000 new postcodes are generated in the UK every year. So, by relying on the website, you could pay SDLT when you don't need to.

As an alternative to the postcode search, you can download a list of all the SDLT disadvantaged areas from the following addresses:

COUNTRY	WEB ADDRESS
England	http://www.hmrc.gov.uk/so/dar/england.pdf
Wales	http://www.hmrc.gov.uk/so/dar/wales.pdf
Scotland	http://www.hmrc.gov.uk/so/dar/scotland.pdf
Northern Ireland	http://www.hmrc.gov.uk/so/dar/nireland.pdf

TIP

If you've bought a property in a disadvantaged area then make sure you haven't paid SDLT by mistake. It may have been missed by your solicitor and the Taxman won't automatically tell you it's exempt. If you find that have paid SDLT by mistake, then ring the Taxman's helpline (0845 6030135) for advice on how to reclaim it.

10.2.7. How to take advantage of "averaging relief"

Problem

To prevent buyers trying to split transcations to avoid SDLT, if you (and persons connected to you) are looking to purchase more than one buy-to-let property from the same vendor (e.g. a developer), the general rule is that the SDLT rate is due on the total consideration (i.e. by adding together all the transactions).

This means that if you buy three properties, each for £250,000, you would pay SDLT at 5% on the whole £750,000 rather than 3 x 1% of £250,000.

Solution

From July 19 2011, you can apply for "averaging" relief so instead of the rate of SDLT being based on the total consideration, it is based on the average consideration, i.e. the aggregate consideration divided by the number of dwellings (subject to a minimum rate of 1%). This relief will only apply to multiple residential property purchases.

NOTE. This relief is not automatic so you will need to claim it on the SDLT land transaction return using relief code 33. Always check the return to ensure your solicitor has claimed it.

10.2.8. So how else can I avoid paying SDLT?

Unfortunately, this is not an easy tax to avoid and, as mentioned in 10.2.7., there is anti-avoidance legislation to prevent "splitting" of transactions to stay below the SDLT thresholds. However, there are schemes that may be able to help (an Internet search will give you more information). Just be aware that if you use one of these schemes you'll probably only see about half of the Stamp Duty saved. The rest will go on fees to the company selling the scheme. If it is later challenged by the Taxman, you'll probably be liable for paying the additional SDLT without any comeback to the scheme provider - read the small print carefully.

10.3.   SDLT ON LEASES

As a property investor, you might think that this isn't particularly relevant to you. However, if you purchase a commercial property personally and then lease it to your company (see 9.3.3.), your company could end up paying SDLT on the lease.

10.3.1.   How is SDLT calculated on the grant of a lease?

SDLT is based on the net present value (i.e. the value in today's money) of all the rent payable under the lease over its full term.

If the net present value (NPV) is less than £125,000 for residential properties or less than £150,000 for commercial properties, then there will be no SDLT to pay.

If the NPV is greater than £125,000 for residential properties or £150,000 for commercial properties, the rate of SDLT is 1% on the excess.

If you have exercised the option to tax on your commercial property (see 9.3.6.), then you also need to include the VAT element as part of the rent payable when calculating the NPV.

Lease premiums also attract SDLT at the same rates as for outright purchases. However, where the lease of a commercial property is also subject to an annual rent of more than £1,000, the exemption for the consideration not exceeding £150,000 does not apply and SDLT is due at 1% on any premium up to £250,000.

10.3.2. How do I calculate the NPV over the term of the lease?

The NPV is the total rent payable over the life of the lease, reduced by an annual discount rate of 3.5% (to take account of inflation). Hence, the NPV of £10,000 due in twelve months' time is £9,662 (£10,000 divided by 103.5%).

Visit http://ldccalculator.hmrc.gov.uk/LDC01.aspx to calculate the NPV of the lease and the SDLT payable.

10.3.3. How can I avoid paying SDLT on leases?

One way of doing this would be to issue a licence instead of a lease - see 9.2.3. for details.

SECTION IV

Overseas property tax issues

11. Moving overseas

11.1. CAN I AVOID TAX BY MOVING OVERSEAS?

Moving abroad and becoming a tax exile is often thought as the ultimate tax avoidance scheme. So can it really work?

You can avoid UK Capital Gains Tax (CGT) on the sale of your UK properties by becoming non-resident here and satisfying the "five year rule" (see 11.1.3.).

NOTE. The UK includes England, Scotland, Northern Ireland and Wales. It does not include the Republic of Ireland, the Channel Islands or the Isle of Man.

To avoid UK CGT, you must not sell the property until the tax year following the one in which you left the UK. So, if you left the UK in the 2012/13 tax year, you could not sell the property until after April 6 2013. If you sell it after you've left the UK, but before the end of the tax year, you will automatically have to pay UK CGT.

11.1.1. How can I become non-resident?

You normally stop being a UK resident from the day after your departure if either:

- you leave for full-time employment abroad for at least a complete tax year (the year that starts on April 6) - provided you spend less than 183 days in the UK in any tax year and your visits to the UK average less than 91 days a tax year, taken over a maximum of four tax years or
- you leave the UK permanently.

WARNING! Following recent tax cases, the Taxman will now look at the overall pattern of residence and ignore the simple day counting. His new approach requires that you make a "distinct break" from the UK. Failure to do so will mean you could still be considered UK resident. But his guidance is clear on one point - if you are in the UK for 183 days or more in any one tax year, you are, without exception, resident in the UK.

NOTE. From April 2013, there is a plan to introduce a statutory test of tax residence to remove the uncertainty but the final details have not yet been released.

Residence test - days of arrival and departure in the United Kingdom

From April 6 2008, any day where the individual is present in the UK at midnight will be counted as a day of presence in the UK for purposes of the residence test.

An exception to this rule is where passengers are transiting through the UK, between two places outside the UK. This exception will apply to individuals who change airports, terminals or between methods of transport when transiting through the UK. Days spent in transit, which could involve being in the UK at midnight, will not be counted as days of presence in the UK provided that whilst in transit the individual does not take part in activities which are not related to the transit, such as attending meetings.

11.1.2. What does leaving the UK permanently actually mean?

To start with, unless you've got a contract to work abroad, you need to leave the UK for an entire tax year. In other words, to be non-resident for CGT purposes, you will have to leave the UK before, say, April 5 2013 and not return until after April 6 2014. You will also need to provide evidence of leaving the UK permanently.

Such evidence would be:

*   buying a property abroad
*   selling or letting out your UK property
*   arranging for all your belongings to be transported abroad.

If you can't provide enough evidence at the start of your absence from the UK, then you will provisionally be treated as remaining resident in the UK for a period of up to three years. If, after three years, your UK visits have averaged less than 91 days a year, the Taxman will generally agree that you were not resident from the date you left the UK.

To summarise, as long as you don't spend more than 90 days a year in the UK after you've left, you will normally be treated as non-resident.

> **TIP**
>
> Once you leave the UK, make sure your trips back don't last more than seven weeks per tax year (April 6 to April 5). Keep your travel documents as proof of your arrival and departure dates.

11.1.3. Do I have to tell the Taxman I'm leaving the UK?

There's no longer a legal requirement to inform the Taxman of your departure from the UK. However, it's still a good idea to complete the form P85 (available at http://www.hmrc.gov.uk/cnr/p85.pdf) explaining where you have gone and how long you expect to be away.

By doing this, the Taxman can't penalise you for not telling him your intentions.

You will also need to complete the "Residence, remittance basis etc." supplementary pages on your self-assessment tax return (available to download from http://www.hmrc.gov.uk/forms/sa109.pdf).

11.1.4. What is the "five-year rule"?

If you sell a property that you owned when you lived in the UK, then you won't be liable to UK CGT as long as you stay non-resident for five full tax years. This means that if you leave the UK before April 5 2013, the earliest you could return would be April 6 2018.

NOTE. You can still sell the property within five years of leaving the UK as long as you make sure you stay non-resident for five years. After that you can return to the UK and there will be no tax to pay.

EXAMPLE

Mark and Val bought an investment property in the UK for £100,000 in October 2004. In July 2011, they emigrated to Spain. A year later, they decided to sell their investment property in the UK for £250,000. Their potential Capital Gains Tax bill is £36,064 (28% x (150,000 - £21,200 annual exemptions)). However, if they stay non-resident in the UK until April 6 2017 (five complete tax years from the date they emigrated) they will have no UK CGT liability.

11.1.5. What happens if I sell my UK property and then return to the UK within five years?

If you sell your property while you are non-resident, but you return to the UK within five years, you will have to pay CGT on the sale of the property in the tax year that you return.

11.1.6. Can the five-year period be reduced?

Before March 16 2005, the five-year period could be considerably reduced if you moved to a country which has a favourable double tax agreement (also known as a double tax treaty) with the UK. These agreements were set up to prevent people from paying tax twice (i.e. in two countries). They usually override UK tax legislation such as the five-year rule, and will often provide that any capital gain will only be taxable in the country where the individual is resident.

However, since March 16 2005, anti-avoidance legislation has been introduced which means that individuals are no longer able to exploit the terms of any Double Taxation Agreement (DTA) to escape UK CGT. So, if you've planning to become non-resident, be aware that you will still have to pay CGT if you return to the UK within five years.

11.1.7. Does the "five-year rule" apply to any gain made on my main home?

Your main residence is exempt from UK CGT for up to three years after you move out (see 5.1.4.). The five-year rule about not returning is therefore not an issue if you sell it within three years.

11.1.8. Will I have to pay CGT in my country of residence?

It wouldn't be much good avoiding UK CGT only to find that you end up paying more tax in your country of residence. So, before you move abroad, you need to find out whether gains on UK property are subject to tax in your proposed country of residence. You also need to check whether these local laws are overridden by the double tax agreement between the UK and your country of residence.

For example, under Spanish domestic law, if you are a Spanish tax resident you are liable to Spanish CGT on a sale of property anywhere in the world. However, this is overridden by (Article 13(1) and Article 24(4) of) the UK-Spain double tax agreement, which states that the country in which the properties are situated is the country which has the right to tax. So, the UK has the right to tax, but under UK domestic tax law, the UK does not tax because you will be non-UK resident. Therefore, you could avoid CGT altogether as long as you stay non-resident for at least five years.

As the CGT rules and rates in each country are different from those in the UK, and the double tax agreements can be quite complicated to interpret, we would advise you to seek advice from an international tax advisor.

> **TIP**
>
> Check the local tax rates on capital gains in the country where you are moving. For example, it wouldn't be worth avoiding UK tax at 28% if you then had to pay 34.5% tax (19% CGT and 15.5% social charges for French residents) on the gain because you were living in France (France's recent treaty with the UK does not protect gains on property in the UK).

11.1.9. Can I be resident nowhere and avoid CGT?

Yes, you can be resident nowhere. For example, you could take up residence on a yacht, sailing around sunnier climes, but not remaining in any one country (including territorial waters) for long enough to become resident in that country.

However, to avoid UK CGT on the sale of your UK properties, you would still need to follow the five-year rule to prevent paying CGT on your return to the UK. So, it would have to be quite a long cruise! Alternatively, you may consider moving to a CGT-free country such as Dubai or The Seychelles.

11.2. CAN I ALSO AVOID INCOME TAX IF I'M NON-RESIDENT?

The rules for taxing income when you're overseas are quite different from the CGT rules. Even if you're no longer resident in the UK, you still have to pay UK tax on your rental income from any properties you own in the UK. This is often deducted at source under the "Non-Resident Landlords Scheme".

However, the personal allowance is usually available in such circumstances so you can still avoid paying tax on your UK rental income if your total UK income is less than £8,105 (2012/13).

11.2.1. What is the "Non-Resident Landlords Scheme"?

As its name suggests, the "Non-Resident Landlords Scheme" is a scheme for taxing the UK rental income of property investors who are not resident in the UK. However, just to be confusing, in this case you will be non-resident if you have been absent from the UK for just six months or more.

The scheme requires UK letting agents to deduct income tax at the basic rate (20% for 2012/13) from any rent collected for non-resident landlords. If you don't have a UK letting agent acting for you, or if a "let-only" service is provided, and the rent is more than £100 a week, then it is your tenant who must deduct the tax.

11.2.2. Can I apply to have my rent received without deduction of tax?

If you are a non-resident landlord and want to receive your UK rents without tax deducted, then you must apply for the Taxman's approval. If successful, a notice of approval will be sent to you and your letting agent or tenant, authorising them to pay your rent without deducting tax. Please note that, even though rent may be paid with no tax deducted, you are still liable to UK tax and, therefore, your rental income must be included on your self-assessment tax return.

Due to the increased administration, most letting agents prefer non-resident landlords to apply for approval to pay rent without tax deducted and will often charge you more if you don't get approval.

To apply for your rents to be received gross, complete form NRL1 which can usually be obtained from your letting agent or by telephoning the HMRC's helpline on 0845 070 0040. Alternatively, you can download the form from http://www. hmrc.gov.uk/cnr/nrl1.pdf. You should then send your completed form to: HMRC, CAR - Personal Tax International, Unit 406, St John's House, Merton Road, Bootle, Merseyside L75 1BB.

11.2.3. Why might my application be unsuccessful?

If you have a poor tax history then your application may be declined. So, before applying, make sure all your tax affairs are up-to-date. Also, note that the Taxman can withdraw his approval if your self-assessment tax return is filed late or you don't pay any tax due on time.

11.2.4. Tax avoidance strategy: how to reduce the tax on your UK rental income

If you're likely to be paying 40% or 50% on your UK rental profits as a non-resident landlord, then you could consider forming an offshore company. A non-UK company owning property in the UK can only be taxed at a maximum rate of 20% (the withholding tax rate). This means you could save up to 30% tax on your rental income.

TRAP. If an offshore company holds a residential property worth more than £2 million then the company faces a 15% SDLT charge when it buys the property. There will also be a CGT charge if the £2 million plus property is sold out of the company. You need to weigh up the cost of these additional taxes against the potential income tax savings.

12. Investing in overseas property

12.1. WHY INVEST IN OVERSEAS PROPERTY?

UK property investors are increasingly turning their attentions to buying property overseas where there is much faster capital growth so they can make a greater return on their investment. Investing in an overseas property can also provide a regular holiday home to enjoy and possibly even a place in the sun to retire to.

So, if you've decided to invest in an overseas property, what are the tax implications?

12.2. HOW IS OVERSEAS RENTAL INCOME TAXED?

If you are a UK resident and own an overseas property that you let out, then your rental profits are normally calculated in much the same way as UK property rental income. You can also take advantage of the furnished holiday home rules if the holiday home is situated in the European Economic Area (EEA) and satisfies the criteria (see 3.2.1.). Unfortunately, however, the furnished holiday home rules never apply to overseas property outside the EEA.

12.2.1. Do I have to pay tax on my overseas income if I'm not UK domiciled (a non-dom)?

Until April 6 2008, if you were resident in the UK, but not UK domiciled, you used to only pay income tax on your overseas rental income as and when the income was moved to your UK bank account (known as the "remittance basis").

However, from April 6 2008, if you've been UK resident but not UK domiciled for at least seven out of the last nine years (preceding the year in which a claim is made) and you want to continue to be taxed on the remittance basis, you have to make a one-off annual payment of £30,000.

Recently, there have been further changes to these rules. From April 6 2012, if you've been UK resident but not UK domiciled for twelve of the last 14 years and you wish to retain access to the remittance basis, you must pay an increased annual charge of £50,000. The current annual charge of £30,000 is retained for those who have been resident for at least seven of the past nine years but fewer than twelve years, and wish to claim the remittances basis.

Overseas property tax issues

The charge applies to adults and so individuals under the age of 18 will not be required to pay the £30,000 until the year in which they turn 18.

Money brought in from an offshore source to pay the charge will not be taxed as a remittance, provided the payment is made directly to the Taxman by cheque or electronic transfer.

Where an individual has un-remitted income or gains which are less than £2,000, that individual can continue to be taxed on the remittance basis without making a claim or without having to pay the £30,000 or £50,000 charge. An individual may also elect to be charged on the remittance basis in one year and not elect in the following year.

Where an individual makes a claim for the remittance basis to apply, that individual will not be entitled to personal allowances for Income Tax purposes or the annual exemption for CGT.

So if you're non-domiciled but resident in the UK and don't want to remit your income to the UK, whether you decide to pay the £50,000 charge depends on your level of income on your overseas income and gains:

Under £2,000 - choose the remittance basis as you won't lose your personal allowances and won't have to pay the charge.

£2,000 to £100,000 - probably better not to choose the remittance basis as it will always be cheaper to pay UK tax on the income and gains than pay the £50,000 charge. And this way, you can also keep your annual exemptions.

£100,000 to £178,572 - if this relates to a gain on overseas property, then it would still be cheaper to pay the UK tax on the gain than pay the £50,000 charge if you are not remitting the income. For example, a gain of £178,000 would result in UK tax of £49,840 (£178,000 x 28%) assuming your CGT allowance has been used against UK gains. However, if it relates mainly to overseas income, then the tax would be £50,000 (£178,000 x 50% = £89,000) so it would be better to pay the charge.

Over £178,572 - if you are not remitting the income to the UK, it may be better to pay the charge as the UK tax on all types of income and gains will be more than £50,000.

12.2.2. Can I change domicile and avoid UK income tax by keeping the income overseas?

Domicile is different from nationality and residence and you can only have one domicile at a time. You are domiciled in the country that is your permanent home even though you may be working and living in another. You normally acquire the same domicile as your father when you are born. So, if your father's permanent place of residence was the UK, you will be domiciled in the UK.

It is very difficult to change your domicile and it would require a permanent move away from your original place of domicile to a new country with the intention of staying there until the end of your days.

However, this works in your favour if you were originally from overseas and are now resident in the UK. Unless you've taken positive steps to change your domicile, you will still be considered domiciled in your country of origin. Therefore, if you have significant overseas income (over £100,000) that you are happy to keep out of the UK, then you should save tax by paying the £50,000 charge instead.

12.2.3. What exchange rate do I use?

When preparing your overseas property accounts, the rental income should be the sterling equivalent of the overseas amount at the date it arises. However, you can simplify the calculation by using an average exchange rate for the year. You can find these rates at http://www.hmrc.gov.uk/exrate/index.htm.

12.2.4. If I've got UK and overseas property, can I group all the income together?

No. You can group all your overseas income together, but it needs to be shown separately from your UK property income. If you own properties in separate overseas countries, then you should prepare individual profit and loss accounts for each country's income. This is because income from different countries may be taxed differently due to different double tax agreements.

12.2.5. Which expenses can I claim against my overseas rental income?

The rules for which expenses you can claim are the same as for UK property income (see 2.1.), i.e. they must be wholly and exclusively for the purposes of your property rental business.

Travelling expenses

A very common question is whether you can claim your flight and other travel costs to your foreign property against your rental income. Unfortunately, you will only be able to claim these expenses if the reason for your trip is exclusively for your property business. This is often very difficult to prove because the Taxman will automatically assume that you're on holiday. Even if a journey is partly for maintaining the property etc., he will deny the relief.

Helen owns a property in Italy. She goes out there for two weeks, partly to do up the property and partly to have a holiday. None of Helen's travel costs will be allowable.

If you want to claim the travel costs, then you will need strong evidence to prove that your trip was purely business. For example, you had to spend three weeks re-decorating the property and any private benefit was purely incidental.

TIP

As all foreign property rentals are treated as one business, you could make a claim for the cost of travel to your loss-making rental property in Spain to carry out some repairs against the rental income from a property in France.

Mortgage interest

There are several ways of raising the cash to buy your overseas property. You could use the property you are buying as security and borrow the money from a foreign bank. Alternatively, you may decide to re-mortgage your UK home to provide the funds to buy abroad. Either way, you can still offset the interest against your overseas rental profits in the same way as you can for UK income (see 2.2.).

Wear and tear allowance

Just to clarify, you can still claim wear and tear allowance against your overseas income as long as the property is fully furnished (see 2.5.1.). The allowance is 10% of the gross rents after deducting any expenses that were borne by you that should normally be borne by a tenant. So, if you pay for any of the following services, they need to be deducted from your gross rental income before calculating the wear and tear allowance:

- cable TV subscription
- telephone rental
- electricity and gas
- cleaning and laundry
- consumables (light bulbs, washing up liquid, toilet rolls etc.)
- refuse collection charges.

12.2.6. What can I do with any loss I make on my overseas rental income?

If you've more than one overseas property, (not including furnished holiday lettings in the EEA which are taxed separately), you can offset the loss you make on one against the profit you make on another in the same tax year.

If that still leaves you with a loss then you can only carry the loss forward and offset it against any future overseas rental profits.

TIP

Where you have substantial losses, it's worthwhile ensuring that your overseas rental business continues by ensuring you always keep an overseas rental property let out.

12.2.7. Where on my tax return do I put the overseas rental income?

Although the income is from property, it doesn't go on the "UK Property" pages (unless it's from a furnished holiday home in the EEA). Instead, you need to complete page F4 of the "Foreign" pages. If this is the first year you have received foreign rental income, you can download the "Foreign" pages from http://www. hmrc.gov.uk/forms/sa106.pdf.

12.2.8. Will I also have to pay tax on the rental income in the country where the property is situated?

Although some countries such as Dubai have no income tax, you will probably have to pay tax on the rental income in most overseas countries. However, you are usually entitled to a credit against your UK tax for any tax that you've already paid in the foreign country. You will be able to get a tax credit if the overseas country has a "double tax agreement" with the UK (see 11.1.6.). So, for example, if you received £5,000 in rental profits from a property in France, then you may have to pay tax on this in France, but you can offset it against your UK tax bill. However, if the foreign tax paid is more than the UK tax due, then the amount you can offset is limited to the amount of UK tax, i.e. you can't claim a refund for the additional foreign tax paid.

The tax rules on what you can deduct from your rental income also vary from country to country. For example, in Portugal you can't include mortgage interest when calculating your rental profits, so you could have a situation where you have made a rental profit on your Portuguese tax return but show a loss on your UK one.

Overseas property tax issues

IV

12.2.9. How do I pay the overseas tax?

You will usually have to complete a tax return in that country and you should therefore seek advice from a local accountant. Many countries will withhold tax from your gross rental income to make sure that you meet your tax liability in that country. This is equivalent to the UK's Non-resident Landlords Scheme (see 11.2.1.).

For example, in Portugal, a withholding tax of 15% will be deducted from your rental income either by the tenant or by a local agent.

12.2.10. Is the tax year the same as in the UK?

No. In most overseas countries the tax year is the same as a calendar year i.e. it runs from January 1 to December 31. Therefore, you may have to prepare two sets of rental accounts, one to complete your UK tax return and one for your tax return in the overseas country.

12.3. HOW ARE CAPITAL GAINS ON OVERSEAS PROPERTIES TAXED?

Unless you are intending to retire overseas, it is likely that at some point you will want to sell the property. Therefore, before buying a foreign property, it is important to consider the CGT implications. There would be no point making a significant capital gain only to see it wiped out by a hefty tax bill.

12.3.1. Is CGT due in the UK on an overseas property?

If you are a UK resident, you have to pay CGT on your worldwide property gains.

12.3.2. How do I calculate the gain when it's in a foreign currency?

The gain is calculated in much the same way as a gain on UK property (see Chapter 4). The gain or loss on the disposal of property abroad is arrived at by comparing the sterling equivalent of the cost at the date of purchase with the sterling equivalent of the proceeds at the date of sale. Unfortunately, you can't take advantage of a favourable exchange rate by working out the gain in the foreign currency and then converting it.

12.3.3. Is CGT due in the overseas country?

Selling a property overseas will usually give rise to a gain in the overseas country as well as in the UK. However, if you had to pay tax in the foreign country, you would be able to offset it against your UK CGT bill.

The calculation for capital gains varies from country to country and you could find that the tax you have to pay in the foreign country is greater than the UK tax due. In this case, the amount of foreign tax you can deduct cannot be more than the UK CGT due and you would effectively be paying the tax rate on the gain in the foreign country.

12.4. WHAT ARE THE INHERITANCE TAX IMPLICATIONS OF OWNING OVERSEAS PROPERTY?

Inheritance Tax (IHT) is due on all your worldwide property as long as you are domiciled in the UK, or deemed UK domiciled for IHT purposes. Someone resident in the UK for at least 17 of the last 20 tax years is deemed UK domiciled for IHT purposes.

Even if you can move abroad permanently and sever sufficient connections with the UK and build up enough connections with your new country, you will still be deemed domiciled in the UK and subject to UK Inheritance Tax on your worldwide assets until the end of the fourth tax year after leaving the UK.

However, estate taxes are normally also due on property in the overseas country and it is usually the foreign country that has the first right to tax. Any foreign tax paid can then be offset against the UK IHT bill.

12.4.1. Forced heirship

You should not presume that a foreign country will recognise your UK will. In some countries, you cannot give your estate away as intended in your will as it is necessary to benefit particular family members. The state actually dictates who can inherit and how much.

France, Italy and Spain all have forced heirship rules and you should seek advice from a legal expert on ways of dealing with this.

12.5. SHOULD I SET UP A LIMITED COMPANY TO INVEST IN OVERSEAS PROPERTY?

There's no definitive answer to this question as it depends on the laws of the country you want to invest in and whether you want to rent it out permanently or occupy the property yourself some of the time.

Property investors set up limited companies for a variety of reasons. For example, to avoid local property taxes in Portugal or forced heirship rules in France. In other countries, local laws do not allow foreign individuals to buy property directly so you may have to set up a company to buy there, e.g. Bulgaria. You should therefore seek advice from an expert in the foreign country's tax system before deciding whether you should set up a limited company.

In the past, if you decided to purchase an overseas property through a company, you had to take care to ensure that an unwelcome UK benefit-in-kind charge did not arise because you or your family also use the property as a holiday home.

However, the Taxman recently scrapped the tax charge as long as the company is owned by individuals, the property is the company's only asset and is used solely by the owner or his family as part of his domestic arrangements.

12.5.1. Can I avoid UK income tax if I set up an offshore company?

This party depends on where the company's management and control are but as a UK resident it will be virtually impossible to avoid tax by setting up an offshore company. If you control the company from the UK, then it will be considered to be a UK resident company. And if it's resident in the UK then it will be subject to UK tax rules.

UK resident company

If a UK resident company owns property abroad, it is liable to Corporation Tax on income received before deduction of foreign taxes, and also on any capital gains on the disposal of foreign properties. A company's income from all property let abroad is treated as the profits of an "overseas property business" and computed in broadly the same way as for individuals, but with the profit or loss computed separately for properties in different countries in order to calculate the amount of any available double tax relief.

Offshore company

Even if the company's management and control are outside the UK, it's likely that the Taxman will still try and tax the income. This is because he has special anti-avoidance provisions that prevent an individual (or his spouse) who is resident in the UK from obtaining a tax advantage by owning properties in an offshore company while he still benefits from the income.

However, these special rules do not apply where the offshore company is set up for genuine commercial reasons and not to avoid tax. Therefore, if you are considering investing in a country such as Bulgaria where you have to set up a company to buy property, then you have a strong argument for saying that the anti-avoidance provisions don't apply and that you shouldn't be taxed on the offshore company's income.

12.5.2. Can I avoid UK CGT if I set up an offshore company?

Special rules also apply to capital gains in offshore companies if the company would be considered a close company (i.e. it has less than five directors/shareholders) if it were a UK resident. A company owned by just you and your spouse would be a close company.

In such a case, if you are UK resident and domiciled, you will be personally taxed on any capital gain in proportion to your shareholding in the company. So having an offshore company doesn't automatically mean you will avoid UK CGT.

Tip 1

The gain apportioned is the gain that would have arisen to the company. This means that you use the company rules to calculate the capital gain - not the rules that apply for individuals. The big advantage to this is that indexation relief is applied to the company's base cost from the date of acquisition to the date of disposal. In a period of high or rising inflation, using an offshore company could be attractive as the indexation allowance could easily outweigh the loss of the £10,600 annual exemption that is available to individuals.

Tip 2

There is a de minims limit of 10%. Therefore, if you club together with family or friends and each own less than 10% of the shares in an offshore company, there would be no need to attribute the capital gains to the shareholders personally.

12.6.   ARE THERE ANY OTHER TAXES THAT I NEED TO CONSIDER?

You need to be fully aware of any other taxes that you may incur on foreign property and again you should seek advice from an expert. There are a raft of other taxes, but two common ones are:

Purchase taxes

Most countries will charge some sort of tax when you purchase a property. For example, in Spain it's generally 7% of the purchase value.

Wealth tax

Some countries charge an annual local wealth tax which is a tax on the value of your assets, e.g. property, held in that country. In France, for example, for non-residents this is calculated on the value of the property after any mortgage. You can reduce the charge significantly by borrowing against the overseas property.

SECTION V

Appendices

APPENDIX A
THE EUROPEAN ECONOMIC AREA

Countries comprising the European Economic Area are as follows:

Austria	Belgium	Bulgaria
Cyprus	Czech Republic	Denmark
Estonia	Finland	France
Germany	Greece	Hungary
Iceland	Republic of Ireland	Italy
Latvia	Liechtenstein	Lithuania
Luxembourg	Malta	The Netherlands
Norway	Poland	Portugal
Romania	Slovakia	Slovenia
Spain	Sweden	UK

APPENDIX B
CLAIMING EARLIER YEAR LOSSES ON SHARES

HM Revenue & Customs

.... *(insert address)*
....
....
....
.... *(insert date)*

Your ref .... *(insert your ten digit tax reference)*

Dear Sirs

Claim for capital losses

In the tax year ended April 5 .... *(insert year)*, I sold .... *(insert figure)* shares in .... *(insert name)* plc for £ .... *(insert figure)*. This resulted in a capital loss of £ .... *(insert figure)*. In accordance with the provisions of Schedule 1AB TMA 1970, I would like to amend my .... *(insert year)* tax return to include this loss on the return and carry it forward to set against future capital gains.

Please could you acknowledge receipt of this claim.

Yours faithfully

....
(insert name)

APPENDIX C
NEGLIGIBLE VALUE CLAIM

HM Revenue & Customs

.... *(insert address)*
....
....
....

.... *(insert date)*

Your ref .... *(insert your ten digit tax reference)*

Dear Sirs

Negligible value claim

I claim relief under s.24(2) of the Taxation of Capital Gains Act 1992 for the tax year ended April 5 .... *(insert year)* in respect of my shareholding in .... *(insert company name)* plc which cost £ .... *(insert figure)*.

*[The shares are included on the "negligible value list" maintained by the Shares Valuation office and were of negligible value as at the date of this claim].

*[The shares are not currently included on the "negligible value list" maintained by the Shares Valuation office, but I believe the shares are of negligible value and would ask the Shares Valuation office to consider including them on the list].

Please could you acknowledge receipt of this claim.

Yours faithfully

....
(insert name)

* *delete as appropriate*

APPENDIX D
PRIVATE RESIDENCE ELECTION

HM Revenue & Customs

.... *(insert address)*
....
....
....

.... *(insert date)*

Your ref .... *(insert your ten digit tax reference)*

Dear Sirs

Private residence election

I acquired a second residence on .... *(insert purchase date)*. In accordance with the provisions of s.222(5) Taxation of Chargeable Gains Act 1992, I hereby elect that the following property should be treated as my main residence with effect from .... *(insert date)*.

.... *(insert address)*

....

....

....

Please could you acknowledge receipt of this election.

Yours faithfully

....
(insert name)

APPENDIX E
VARIATION OF PRIVATE RESIDENCE ELECTION

HM Revenue & Customs

.... *(insert address)*
....
....
....

.... *(insert date)*

Your ref .... *(insert your ten digit tax reference)*

Dear Sirs

Variation of private residence election

I have currently elected that .... *(insert address)* should be treated as my main residence for Capital Gains Tax purposes. In accordance with the provisions of s.222(5) Taxation of Chargeable Gains Act 1992, I now wish .... *(insert address)* to be regarded as my main residence with effect from .... *(insert date)*.

Please could you acknowledge receipt of this election.

Yours faithfully

....
(insert name)

APPENDIX F
PROPERTY MANAGEMENT COMPANY CONTRACT

CONTRACT FOR MANAGEMENT SERVICES

This agreement is made on .... *(insert date of agreement)* between

(1) ....*(insert property management company name)* (the "Company")

and

(2) .... *(insert property owner name)* (the "Property Owner")

FINDING TENANTS

The Company will find a suitable tenant for the Property Owner for a fee of .... *(insert figure)*. This fee must be paid upon commencement of the tenancy. The service will include: continuously and vigorously advertising your property until it has been let to a suitable tenant. Placing advertisements in newspapers. Interviewing and vetting all suitable prospective tenants and taking them to view the property. Taking up references from all tenants and supplying contracts.

ONGOING MANAGEMENT SERVICE

For .... *(insert figure)* of the rental payment over the period of the Tenancy Agreement, the Company will carry out the following services on behalf of the Property Owner:

• rent collection

• notification to service companies at the commencement of the tenancy e.g. gas, electric, water council tax

• arrangement and supervision of minor repairs to the property and general maintenance.

ADDITIONAL SERVICES

Inventory

The Company will charge a fee of .... *(insert figure)* for preparing an inventory. This includes compiling and inventory for three bedrooms, two reception areas, kitchen and bedroom. For each additional room or out house there will be an extra charge of .... *(insert figure)*.

Renewal

If the original tenancy is extended for the same tenant or occupier, a further charge will become payable to the Company at the outset of such extended periods at the rate of .... *(insert figure)* of the rental payable during extended period.

Inspections

The Company will make quarterly inspections during the period of letting to ensure the premises are being use in an appropriate manner. The charge will be .... *(insert figure)* per inspection.

Signed on behalf of the Company   ....

Name (in capitals)   ....

Position   ....

Signed by the Property Owner   ....

Date   ....

APPENDIX G
LICENCE

In respect of .... *(insert address)*

THIS LICENCE is made on .... *(insert date)*

Between

.... *(insert name)*, ("the Licensor")

and

.... *(insert Company name)*, ("the Licensee")

The Licensor and the Licensee have agreed to occupation of the premises known as .... *(insert property address)* on the following terms:

1. The licence to run for a term of .... *(insert term)* commencing on .... *(insert start date)* and expiring on .... *(insert finish date)*. At the end of the Licence the Licensee will offer vacant possession if a formal renewal has not been completed.

2. The Licence fee to be £ .... *(insert figure)* per month, payable in advance calendar monthly by standing order. This fee is exclusive of all non-domestic and water rates and all other outgoings and is payable from the .... *(insert start date)*.

3. The Licensor reserves the right to increase or decrease the licence fee at his discretion. The Licensor will give the Licensee reasonable written notice of any significant increase or decrease in the fees payable.

4. The Licensee to maintain and give up on termination of the Licence the interior of the premises in as good and substantial repair and decoration as exists before this Licence commences and the Licensee upon notice shall immediately attend to necessary repairs.

5. The Licensee to comply with any enactments or regulations or such like which may be required from any competent Authority.

6. The Premises are not to be used other than for normal .... *(insert office/ manufacturing etc.)* purposes in connection with the Licensee's proposed business. The Licensee is not to do or permit anything to be done on the premises which is illegal.

7. The Licensee to insure and keep insured the premises against loss by fire and such other perils.

8. The Licensee to permit the Licensor at any reasonable time to enter the premises.

9. The Licensee to indemnify and keep indemnified the Licensor against all actions, claims and demands arising from the Licensee's use and occupation of the premises.

10. At any time within the term of the Licence, the Licensee or Licensor may give one calendar month's notice to terminate this Licence.

11. By signing this agreement, the Licensee formally acknowledges that this is a Licence only and no tenancy is created, whether formal or informal.

Signed for the Licensor: ....

Name: .... *(insert your name)*

Date: ....

Signed for the Licensee: ....

Name: .... *(insert Company name)*

Date: ....

APPENDIX H
CAPITAL ALLOWANCES ELECTION

Notification of an Election to use an alternative apportionment in accordance with s.198 Capital Allowances Act 2001, Section 198 between .... *(insert name of seller)* and .... *(insert name of buyer)*.

Property address:

Interest *(freehold/leasehold):*

Seller's name and address:

Tax district and reference:

Buyer's name and address:

Tax district and reference:

Date of completion of sale:

Amount apportioned to machinery and plant fixtures (£):
(see attached for details)

Sale price *(£)*:

The seller and the buyer hereby jointly elect, pursuant to the provisions of s.198 Capital Allowances Act 2001, that the amount of the sale price to be treated as capital expenditure on plant and machinery incurred by the buyer on the provision of the fixtures is .... *(insert amount as above)*. A list of the fixtures is given on the next page.

Signed:...

Name of seller: ....

Date: ....

For and on behalf of.. *(insert name of the seller)*

Signed:...

Name: ....

Date: ....

For and on behalf of .... *(insert name of the buyer)*

Example:

Schedule of Plant and Machinery to be included in s.198 Election

.... *(insert address)*

ITEM	APPORTIONED AMOUNT
Ventilation	£4,500.00
Blinds	£1,500.00
Total	**£6,000.00**

CLAUSES FOR CONTRACT

1. Have any of the Fixtures included in the transaction been included in an election either under s.198 or s.199 Capital Allowances Act 2001 or s.59B of the Capital Allowances Act 1990? If so, please provide a copy of such election notice(s).

2. If requested by us, will you enter into an agreement with us to make an election under s.198 or s.199 of the Capital Allowances Act 2001?

Notes

Notes

Notes

Notes

Notes

Notes

Notes

Notes

Notes